THE ADVENTURE BOOK OF STARS

The Adventure Book of
STARS

THOMAS D. NICHOLSON, ASTRONOMER

AMERICAN MUSEUM—HAYDEN PLANETARIUM

Edited by ALFRED D. BECK, Supervisor of Science

Jr. High Schools, N.Y.C. BOARD OF EDUCATION

Illustrated by MILDRED WALTRIP

CAPITOL PUBLISHING COMPANY, INC.

Distributed by GOLDEN PRESS, INC.

To my wife, Branca

Library of Congress Catalog Card Number 58-8459

COPYRIGHT © 1958 BY CAPITOL PUBLISHING COMPANY, INC.
Published by Capitol Publishing Company, Inc.
New York, New York
Manufactured in the United States of America

Fourth printing 1960

Contents

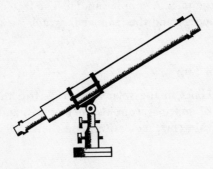

The author wishes to express his deep appreciation to the following for permission to reproduce their photographs:

AMERICAN MUSEUM-HAYDEN PLANETARIUM, p 49, 59, 63, 73, 89; MT. WILSON and PALOMAR OBSERVATORIES, p. 48, 61, 72, 74, 83, 85, 91, 104, 105, 106, 107; YERKES OBSERVATORY, p. 87.

Dear Reader:

I do a good many jobs as an Astronomer at the American Museum-Hayden Planetarium in New York. Among other duties, I teach, lecture, supervise the technical staff, and plan exhibits. Best of all, I like to lecture — to tell people about the stars. I guess I have talked to over half a million persons about the stars.

You see, there is only one way really to know the stars — that is to watch them and use them. I learned them first as a navigator on ships sailing all over the world. You can learn them by doing the things I have suggested in this book.

I hope you will like my book. If you do, then you should be as grateful as I am to the man who helped me a good deal in preparing it, Mr. Alfred D. Beck, Science Supervisor of the Junior High Schools of New York City. As the editor of this book, he has helped me to plan it and has made many valuable suggestions based on his long experience with young people.

Of course, I cannot tell you everything about the stars, the sun, the moon, and the planets in just one book. But I have tried to explain some things that will get you excited about astronomy, excited enough to learn from the sky itself. I want you to have the pleasure from the stars that I have had — the personal adventure of discovery.

THOMAS D. NICHOLSON

1 Man Jumps Into Space

Sometime on the night of October 4, 1957, a giant rocket left its launching pad somewhere in Russia. The huge machine lifted itself slowly, balancing on a long shaft of flame. Swiftly and surely, it sped upward, finally roaring out of sight in a long, graceful arc toward the east. It must have been a beautiful sight to the scientists and workers who watched it. They were actually making history. They were the only ones who knew what was happening. However, within a few hours, the world knew their secret.

By the next morning, almost everyone knew about the launching of the world's first man-made satellite, Sputnik I. Radios around the world were picking up the strange "beep-beep-beep" of the signal coming from the object. It sped around the world hundreds of miles up, completely circling the earth in a little more than an hour and a half. You may have heard the signal on your radio or television set or maybe you were able to tune it in on a short wave receiving set. Within a few days, you could have seen the object, like a bright planet drifting rapidly through the skies. For over three months, it continued to circle and millions of people watched it.

A month later, on November 5, 1957, the Russians launched their second satellite, this one carrying a living occupant, the famous dog, Laika. Then, on February 1, 1958, the first American satellite, Explorer, was launched by the United States Army, with its Jupiter-C rocket. The American satellite travelled higher and farther, and was destined to remain in space far longer than either of the two Russian Sputniks.

The age of space has begun. You probably know this and have looked into the sky with new wonder and interest. Now you realize that some day the things you see there will be explored by men. For many years, people have heard about the possibility of exploring space. Most considered it an idea which belonged in science fiction stories until the Sputniks and Explorer were launched. Then they began to feel that there was something real about this talk of space travel. How is it possible to shoot great rockets so fast and so far? Do you know why the satellite remained in space and did not at once fall back to earth? What kind of journey do you suppose it would be to go out into space?

Travel in space became possible when men learned a new way to use rockets. Rockets go places because something inside the rocket leaves it in a hurry. This is an action followed by a reaction. The principle of reaction is an old one. It was known to the ancient Chinese who shot off simple rockets hundreds of years ago. However the first scientific explanation was given to us by Sir Isaac Newton, in the middle of the 17th century. He described it in his book, *Laws of Motion*. One of these laws stated that "for every action, there is an equal and opposite reaction." It means that every force is matched by an equal force in the opposite direction. This is seldom noticed because usually when we exert a force we push against solid objects, which absorb the reaction.

Have you ever had an experience with the principle of reaction? If you have ever stepped out of a rowboat, you know what reaction can do. The rowboat reacted in the direction opposite to your foot as you tried to step out. As you moved in one direction, by pushing against the boat with your foot, the boat reacted to that force by moving in the opposite direction. At such times if you are not careful, you may be more suprised than pleased by this simple reaction.

More than twenty years ago airplane designers saw new uses for the reaction principle. They developed the reaction motor, which first appeared in jet airplanes during World War II. These jets gulp in great amounts of oxygen from the earth's atmosphere. The engine or motor mixes the oxygen with a combustible fuel and produces an explosion from the mixture. The explosion takes place in a chamber which is open only at the rear of the airplane. Since the front of the firing chamber is closed, the explosion pushes against it and the airplane reacts by moving forward.

Jet engines can work only in the air and not in empty space. Jet engines need the air as a supply of oxygen. They cannot be flown too high because they may run into air that has too little oxygen to support the explosion of the fuel in the firing chamber. Jets which fly at high altitudes use a good deal of their energy simply in compressing the very thin air in order to make an explosion in the firing chamber.

The rocket engine is simpler than a jet engine because it does not need oxygen from the air. It carries its own oxygen. If the fuel is solid, it is mixed with a material which contains oxygen. If the fuel is a liquid, the rocket must carry another liquid which contains the oxygen. Liquid oxygen (lox) may be used. When the two liquids are mixed in the firing chamber of the rocket, burning begins instantly upon contact. The burning goes on so rapidly that it is really a continuous explosion. This explosion pushes against the front wall of the firing chamber, just as in a jet, forcing the rocket to move.

Since the rocket carries its own supply of oxygen, it can operate beyond the limits of the air. This makes it an ideal vehicle for space flight. A rocket actually goes better outside of the atmosphere where there is no resistance to the escape of the gases. The action of these very hot gases, shooting back out of the opening in the firing chamber, is matched by a similar reaction of the gases inside the chamber pushing against the forward wall of the chamber. The faster these gases travel, the faster the rocket will travel. When it is in space, with no air to resist its motion, the rocket will go very fast indeed.

Since a rocket must carry along all of its fuel and the oxygen to burn that fuel, it is very heavy at the start of its flight. This weight is so great that the rocket cannot carry along much extra weight. Yet it is this extra weight which makes up the payload of instruments or passengers that the rocket is designed to transport.

To get the best use out of a rocket the experts have developed the "step rocket." In a "step rocket," several rockets are mounted, one on top of another. After the first rocket has used up all its fuel, it is detached in flight, and the motor of the second rocket begins to burn. Since this second rocket is already travelling very fast, it adds its own speed to the speed it got from the first stage.

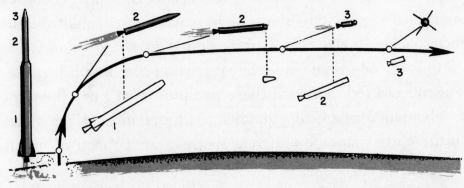

The second part of the rocket can go faster for another reason. It does not have to carry the heavy weight of the enormous empty tanks of the first section which is detached before the second stage begins to fire. After the fuel in the second stage section is used up, this also is detached before the third stage motor begins to burn. Again dead weight is reduced and the third stage is able to go even faster. The third stage may carry the "payload," or a fourth stage. By the time all of the rocket stages have speeded it up, the payload is going fast enough to travel around the earth as a satellite.

This principle of building rocket sections in stages was used to launch the artificial satellites of the United States and the Russians. Although we are not certain, we believe that the Russian Sputniks were launched by three-stage rockets. The U.S. Army Jupiter-C rocket, which launched the first American satellite, used four stages. The U.S. Navy's rocket built to launch the Vanguard satellite uses a three-stage vehicle.

Rockets are being used for many different purposes today. Some of them are designed to be military weapons. Other rockets are being used for research purposes. These rockets carry instruments in their nose as the payload, instead of bombs. Rockets have been fired in this manner up to about 4,000 miles above the earth. Still other rockets have been designed to launch satellites. Their payloads are small instrument-packed metal chambers designed to travel around the earth for a long time while they report on conditions in space. The rocket used to launch these satellites must carry them up to about 300 miles, aim them in a direction nearly parallel to the earth's surface and release them at a speed of about 18,000 miles per hour.

After a rocket has released a satellite in the right way, the things that happen to the satellite thereafter depend on certain natural laws. There is no more rocket power to change its height, speed or direction. There is no air to slow it down. So it obeys the law that an object will remain in motion in a

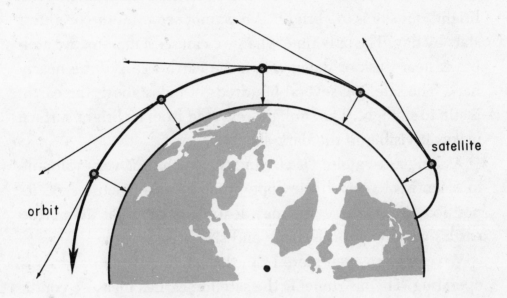

straight line unless acted upon by some other force. Thus it continues to move but not in a straight line. The earth's force of gravitation makes the satellite "fall" toward the earth's center. This is the force which keeps the satellite from flying off into space. The combination of its fast motion and the "fall" produced by the earth's gravitation are just enough to make it circle the earth.

If the satellite is going a little too fast or too slow at the time it is set free, or if it is tilted up or down just a little bit, then it will not travel in a circle. Then it will travel in an ellipse, a slightly oval path like the moon's orbit around the earth. In this way the satellite travels in a path which takes it farthest from the earth at one point and closest at another. All of those launched so far have travelled in this manner.

15

While a satellite is travelling around the earth, you have some opportunity to see it. We cannot see these objects at night, because they are in the earth's shadow, and they are dark. In the daytime, when the satellite is in sunlight and bright, our sky is too bright. We cannot see even the brightest stars by day. The only time when we can see a man-made satellite is near dusk or dawn. Then the earth and sky are nearly dark. The satellite, several hundreds of miles above the earth, is still in sunlight. The sunlight reflected from its bright surface makes it visible in the dark sky.

As long as a satellite is circling the earth, it is very valuable to scientists. Special telescope cameras take pictures of its position. From these we may learn a great deal about the earth's gravity and the shape and size of the earth.

We can learn even more from the satellite while its radio is operating. The instruments the satellite carries measure conditions in space and send us reports by radio. From them we learn the temperature inside and outside the satellite and the amount of cosmic dust which strikes it. Special instruments are used also to measure the amount of ultra-violet energy coming from the sun, to count the cosmic rays, and to measure the strength of the earth's magnetic field. When a satellite carries a living being, as Sputnik II did, then other instruments report its heartbeat, breathing, blood pressure, and body temperature.

The radio signals coming from the Sputniks were very strong "beep-beep-beeps." The ones coming from our Explorer sounded like a loud, throbbing, steady tone. Both kinds of signals have codes built into them which tell scientists about conditions in space. This information helps us to understand more about the earth and the energy coming to it through space.

Science also must learn about conditions in space to find out if it is safe for men to be there. Extreme temperatures, cosmic rays, and ultra-violet rays can kill human beings. Satellites will tell scientists how dangerous these conditions are and perhaps suggest ways to protect the crews of space ships. From what we have learned with satellites, it appears that men may have less to fear than we expected. The cosmic rays, meteoroids, and ultra-violet rays measured so far by the satellites would not have hurt anyone inside the satellites. Even the temperatures have remained fairly comfortable.

Before men can travel safely into space, a great deal more research will be necessary. Now a satellite must remain in space until the very slight air found there slows it down a bit. Then it is destroyed, either by burning like a meteor or by crashing to the earth. We do not want that to happen to a ship carrying a man. Before the first men are sent into space by the United States, we will have to be fairly sure that they will come back safely. In the meantime, of course, we will continue to experiment with satellites and to find out more about space.

Satellites can be expected to do very important things for mankind in the future. Some now being planned will study the earth's weather. Others may bring long distance television to your home. Satellites may be used to relay communications, radio, telephone, or television between places very far apart. The age of satellites has just begun, and so also has the age of space. Someday you will see men travelling into space and returning safely to earth. You may be one of them or you may be one of the scientists who will work out the plans or build the equipment for journeys like that.

Man in space will have an unusual kind of life. Many of the things he is used to on earth will be completely changed. His quarters will be cramped and his supply of food, water, and air will be limited. Once he is in space he will be travelling at great speeds but he will not feel his motion. He will have trouble knowing up and down for there is no up and down in space. The man who jumps into space will have no gravity to guide his senses and to control his movements or the movements of anything in his space craft.

From the moment he takes off from the earth, the space-man of the future will have great problems. The take-off, riding in the top of a gigantic multi-stage rocket launcher, will strain his nerves and strength. Imagine yourself on such a journey, perhaps on a trip to the moon. Let's see what kind of a space traveller you would make.

Days and weeks before the journey, you would go to school. You would need years of training in mathematics, physics, biology, and astronomy. You would learn all about the rocket ship, how to use its equipment, and how to make your journey. The take-off would be controlled by technicians on the ground at the launching site but after that you would have to control everything. Your life would depend on your skill.

Finally, the day of take-off would come. You would probably find yourself in the control room of your ship lying flat on your back on a well-padded couch, to absorb the enormous thrust of the rocket motors. Through earphones, you hear the control officer go through the check-off in the count-down. There would probably be an emergency cord in your hand to allow you to signal the block-house and stop the launching if anything seemed to be going wrong.

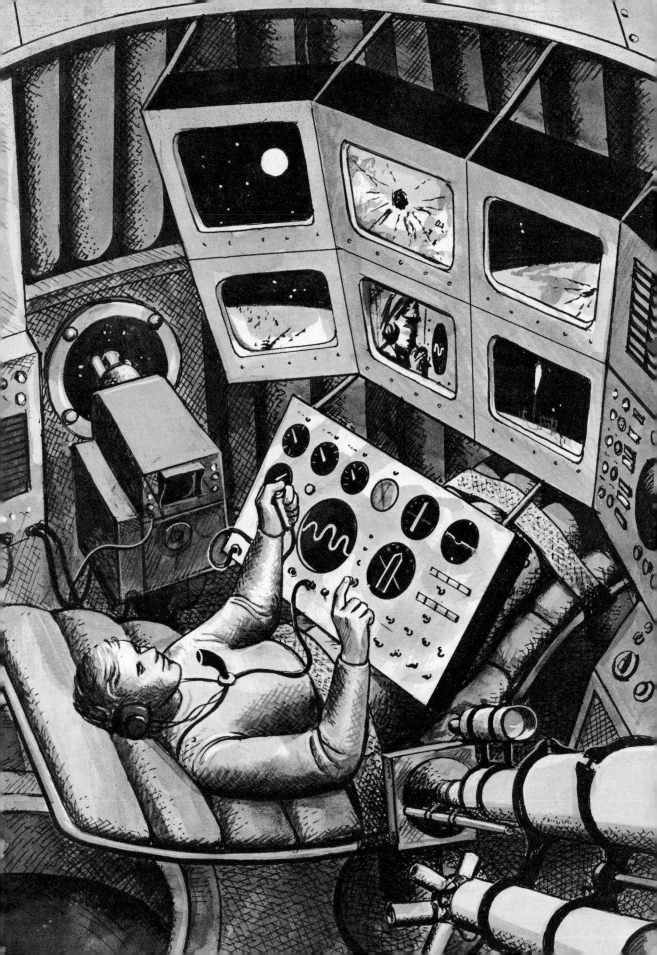

And then, if all went well, the order to blast-off would be given. The whole rocket would vibrate madly with the power of the huge motors in the first stage. Through the frame of the ship you would hear the roar of the explosion in the rocket chamber. Then you would be pressed back into your couch as the huge rocket took off slowly, straight up toward the sky.

Gently at first, then more and more rapidly, the rocket would pick up speed. You would feel yourself pressed down harder and harder, until it would seem that you must weigh several tons. Then suddenly the sound would end, the rocket would be travelling faster than the speed of sound. You would no longer hear the roar of the exhaust. Just as suddenly, the pressure against the couch would end, the first stage motor would quit as it ran out of fuel. You would feel as though you were floating and only the straps across your legs and chest would hold you to your couch.

A moment later, and a terrific thrust from the motors of the second stage would jolt you back against your couch again with even greater force. But you would not hear the second stage motors. At the speed of your rocket ship, they would leave their sound far behind in space. The only sound would come through your earphones as you heard the firing control officer describe the flight of the ship as it was being tracked by telescopes and radar.

Meantime, you would have been quite busy. A regular sequence for reading all of the control instruments in your cabin would have been worked out carefully before the launching. Your job would be to report these readings and all the other things you observed.

After another period of floating and another feeling of being pressed back once more into your couch, you would know that the second stage had been detached and the third stage motors had begun to fire.

At last the fuel in the third stage would be used up, the pressure would end, the third stage would detach, and you would be free in space. Pressing a switch, you would move your pilot's chair to a sitting position closer to the control panel. But you would not release the straps holding you to it, for without them you might float around the tiny cabin. The straps hold you in place and there is no need to release them because the cabin has been designed with everything you need within reach.

Now the careful routine you have practiced begins. Periods of rest, periods of eating, regular radio talks with the earth, and navigation sessions follow a time table. There are also periods of recreation in your schedule. Books, movies, and games help you to relax on the long days of the trip. But mostly you will think about the adventure ahead of you.

You may be heading for a landing on the moon. Maybe you are equipped to step out of your ship and explore the moon's surface. Perhaps the moon is only the first stop on your journey to Mars or Venus. If so, it will be months before you return to the earth.

No one knows when this new age of space will end. For you it will start when you look into the sky and wonder about the things you see there. Now you can begin your own adventure into space by looking into the heavens and learning about sky objects as you watch them. When you do that, you are starting your own "adventures unlimited."

You know your home address but do you know your correct address in space, that is, in the universe? By the time you have read the next few pages you will know the answer. The secret is to be found in the science called astronomy. If you had tried to study astronomy five hundred years ago or more, it would not have been possible. There really was no science of astronomy, as we know it today.

This doesn't mean that people didn't know a good deal about the stars then. They did; they knew some facts about them better than we do now, at least better than most of us. Until our modern age of cities with their lights and haze, of radio, of television and movies, people spent much more time outdoors than we do now. So they had more chances to see what went on in the sky and to become familiar with the things that were there.

Besides, they didn't have some of the modern conveniences that we take for granted, like clocks, calendars, and compasses, and like road maps and street signs. So they *had* to know the stars, and know how the sun and stars moved. Their clock, calendar, and compass were in the sky. The sun and the stars told them the time of day, and the seasons of the year. They looked to the sky for the direction to their destination when they travelled.

Modern astronomers are concerned with what the stars are, where they are in space, what makes their light, and the life history which they follow. The beginning of modern astronomy can be dated with what is sometimes called the Copernican Revolution. The name comes from Nikolaus Copernicus (Kuh-*per*-nih-kus), a Polish churchman and astronomer who died in 1543. Until his time, nearly everyone thought that the earth was the center of the universe and the sun, planets, and stars moved around the earth. But Copernicus believed, and taught and wrote that the earth moves around the sun. Copernicus couldn't prove his theory for he had no telescope. We know today that he was right when he described the earth as a spinning world moving through space around the sun. Because he upset a wrong idea that men had

23

believed for thousands of years, we date from him and from his time the beginning of modern astronomy.

After Copernicus, came many great men of other nations who were able to prove what he could only believe.

These Men Discovered the Proofs for Our Ideas
About the Universe

KEPLER (German, 1571-1630)............discovered the laws controlling the planets as they revolve around the sun.

GALILEO (Italian, 1564-1642)............Built and used the first astronomical telescope.

BRADLEY (English, 1692-1762)..........proved that the earth revolved around the sun.

FRAUNHOFER (German, 1787-1826)....discovered how to tell what the sun and stars were made of.

HALE (American, 1868-1938)............built the 100-inch telescope at Mount Wilson and made the plans for the 200-inch Palomar telescope.

HUBBLE (American, 1889-19....)..........proved that there were galaxies beyond the Milky Way. Also proved that galaxies were expanding.

What kind of universe is this that astronomers have discovered with their telescopes? Well, it begins with the earth and ends somewhere that has not yet been found. Do not make the mistake made by the ancients and the people before Copernicus. The earth—in spite of the fact that we live on it and see the universe from it—is not the center of the universe. As a matter of fact, the earth isn't very important at all in the whole plan of the universe, except, of course, that we *do* live on it.

You may find it easier to understand how the universe is designed if you divide it up into four sections. It is not really divided that way, but this plan will help you keep things in order. So let us divide up the universe into four sections that we will call the *foreground,* the *middleground,* the *background*, and the *extreme background.*

The *foreground* of the universe is the part of space closest to us; the earth and its atmosphere. The earth is like a ball, but a little flat at the top and bottom and bulging out a little around the middle. It is so nearly like a ball that the globes we use as models for it look like perfect spheres.

The earth would look just about the same from space, unless we measured it exactly. It measures 7,927 miles across through the middle, where the equator is, and 27 miles less from pole to pole. The distance around the world is very close to 25,000 miles. Its *total* weight is 6,000,000,000,000,000,000,000 tons. Of the earth's surface, 30% is made of rock, soil, and sand, while 70% is water. Under the surface, there is a layer of

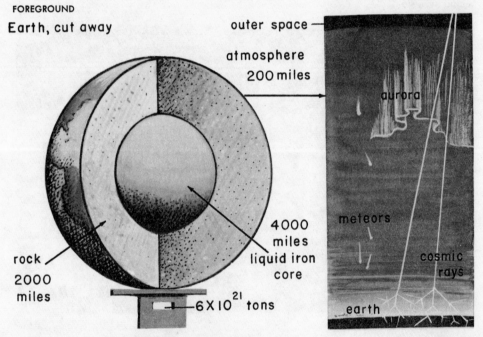

FOREGROUND
Earth, cut away

outer space

atmosphere
200 miles

aurora

rock
2000
miles

4000
miles
liquid iron
core

6×10^{21} tons

meteors

cosmic
rays

earth

rock some 2,000 miles thick and at the center is a hot, liquid core 4,000 miles across, of iron, made very dense by the weight of rock above.

Many of the things you see in the sky are actually in the air, part of the foreground in astronomy. The light of the sun, scattering, reflecting, and bending as it passes through the air, causes the blue light and color of the day, the glow and colors of twilight, rainbows, halos (rings around the sun), and several other strange things. Without the air above us, there would never be any light or color in the sky, even when the sun is up. Many things which bombard the earth from space shoot through the air. You can see some of them, but others cannot be seen.

Next outward from the earth and the air, in this universe in which you live, is the *middleground*, the part of the universe in

MIDDLEGROUND

which the earth belongs. We call it the solar system, the family of the sun. It consists of a large family of objects that circle around the star we call the sun.

The solar system extends out into space perhaps ten billion miles from the sun, or even more. Surrounding it, there are billions of miles of space with nothing in it, nothing but the thinly scattered gas and dust of space. Then, beyond these vast stretches of emptiness, is the *background* in astronomy, the region of the stars. The nearest star is some 25,000 billion miles from our sun. Others are hundreds and even thousands

BACKGROUND

of times farther away. They are found in all directions extending out for many thousands of billions of miles, but they do not extend out forever.

The stars we see in our sky are arranged in the universe like a giant wheel, measuring about 600,000,000 billion miles across and about 60,000,000 billion miles thick. This wheel of stars is called our Galaxy, or sometimes the Milky Way. There are about 100 billion stars in it, and we live there too. Our sun is one of these stars, deep in the midst of it. When you look into the sky at night, you see the Milky Way, a band of hazy light stretching across the heavens. You are looking along the rim of our wheel-like Galaxy, where the stars seem more numerous.

Far beyond the stars of our Galaxy and the nearly empty

space that surrounds them, is the *extreme background,* stretching out as far as astronomers have been able to penetrate with their great telescopes. In it there are many other galaxies like our Milky Way, each made up of billions of stars. There are hundreds of millions of these distant galaxies in deep space, separated by vast distances of near emptiness. The nearest galaxy to the one in which we live is some 15,000,000,000 billion miles from us. The most distant ones we can detect are about 1,000 times further away. Many more galaxies may exist beyond those, but we are not able to see their faint light even with our best modern telescopes.

You see, the universe that has been discovered is indeed vast, but it is also simple in plan. It is made up of space in which there are things called galaxies, great collections of billions of stars. And our sun, with all the stars we see in our sky, belongs to one of these galaxies, the one we call the Milky Way. The earth is simply a small planet which revolves around one of these stars, the sun. This is your address in space.

3 Go Outdoors and Look

Have you ever been confused by some very ordinary thing that appeared in the sky? Perhaps you remember something in your own experience that was very simple to explain but which caused excitement among people by the thousands.

There was the time during World War II when a whole convoy of troop ships with their escort vessels had all of its guns trained on the planet Venus for almost an hour. At last some navigator figured out that it was not some new secret weapon of the enemy. It was just Venus, shining in the clear daytime sky at a time when it was near its greatest brightness. Venus often causes excitement among people. It becomes a very bright evening star quite often—about every year and a half. Then it shines before sunset and during the early evening. Every time it does, countless people are startled or puzzled by it.

The trouble is that people just do not observe things in the sky often enough. If you wish to know something about the sun, the moon, the stars and the planets, the very first thing you should do is to get into the habit of looking into the sky as often as you can.

You should also make it a habit to try to remember some of the things you see there. A good way to do this is to keep a record of what you see and how it behaves, a kind of sky log.

By day you can watch the sun as most everyone knows. But do not look at it directly without very dark glasses—much darker than sun glasses. There are also other things to observe. The moon appears in the daytime sky quite often, and, as those frightened sailors found out, sometimes the planet Venus can be seen. But unless you climb some very high mountain, do not expect to see the stars. They are there, but they are not bright enough to be seen in the daytime.

Everyone knows that the sun rises and sets each day. But not everyone knows just how it happens, how the sun moves from sunrise to sunset, and how that movement changes through the year. Do you? These are the things that you can observe about the sun with ease. To begin with, you might watch the place where the sun rises or sets on a certain day. Then watch where this happens several days later. Do this again and again for a few weeks. Keep notes, using the same tree or other landmark to help you to remember where the sun rose or set. You should also note what time sunrise or sunset took place. After several observations, you will see that the sun does not rise or set in the same place or at the same time day after day. You will certainly learn that the sun does not always rise in the east and set in the west.

You might also observe how high the sun gets at its highest point during the day, which occurs around noontime. But remember our warning not to look directly at the sun. You can use your fist for a measuring stick. Hold it out in front of you and see how many fists there would be between the horizon and the sun. The distance from the horizon to the point over-

head, called the zenith (*zee*-nith), is measured in degrees like an angle and is called altitude. The altitude of the zenith is 90 degrees. When your fist is stretched out in front of you, it covers about 10 degrees of the sky. There should be about 9 fists from the horizon to the point overhead. The altitude of the sun will be the number of fists, or parts of fists, that you measure from the horizon to the point where the sun is located.

If you measure the height of the sun this way several times during the day, you will see that it is highest at noon. If you measure its altitude at noon of each day, you will see that it changes. If you live in the United States or Canada, you will certainly observe that the sun is never overhead. If you tell some people this, it will surprise them. You will also see that the sun is much higher in the sky at noon in the spring than in the winter, and even higher in the summer. Your record of the sun's altitude at noon will show changes through the year. Together with your record of the number of hours that the sun remains above the horizon, these facts will help you to understand why it is colder in winter and warmer in summer.

You should look for the moon in the daytime, too. When you see it, you can make at least five observation records as follows: (1) where it rises or sets, (2) what time it rises or sets, (3) how far from the sun it is located, (4) how its shape changes from day to day and (5) in which direction the "horns," or tips, of the moon point with respect to the sun. If you keep this record of the shape of the moon and its motion in the sky, soon you will know a good deal about it.

The only time you see the moon in the morning sky will be after the full moon. Day after day, from about the second to tenth day following a night when the moon is full, you will be able to see the moon on your way to school in the morning. Each day it will seem to be closer and closer to the sun, and becoming less of a circle of light. Then, for about a week, you will not be able to see the moon at all in the daytime. After that, it will start appearing close to the sun in the afternoon sky first as a small crescent of light. Each day thereafter, you will see it for a longer time. It will seem to have moved farther from the sun, and it will grow larger in area again becoming almost a circle of light. When the moon is full, it will not appear at all while the sun is up. You can see it in the twilight after sunset and before sunrise. Observing the moon like this will (a) help you to understand much better the things you learn about it from books, and (b) make it a very useful guide for you in the sky because its changes in appearance and position follow a regular schedule.

After sunset, there are a good many other things you can see in the sky. The planets that appear at night are usually brighter than the stars and they are the first objects to become visible as darkness approaches. These objects are known as the "evening stars," although they are not stars at all. You can recognize them by the steadiness of their light. They do not appear to twinkle as stars do, although, under certain conditions of the atmosphere, the planets can twinkle also.

Later, as the sky grows darker, the stars begin to appear. At this time, by watching the sky, you can learn one of the secrets of navigators. A navigator is a person who guides a ship to a harbor or an airplane to a landing field. You can observe that the stars grow brighter as the earth and sky darken. Soon you can see the stars, but you cannot see the earth clearly. If you observe carefully, you will notice that there are about 10 to 15 minutes when it is already dark enough to see the stars, but it is still light enough to see the horizon. The same thing is true in the twilight of the morning. These are the times when navigators must observe the stars. They must be able to see the horizon and the stars at the same time in order to measure the altitude of the stars. Only during these two brief periods are the stars useful to navigators at sea.

You might try observing how long twilight lasts. It is from the time sunset takes place until the sky gets completely dark. To measure the time of complete darkness, you should pick out some familiar object and consider the sky completely dark when you can no longer see it. Keep a record, and you will see that twilight does not last the same period each night. It becomes longest at the beginning of summer and winter, and is shorter at the beginning of spring and autumn.

When the sky becomes completely dark, there is no end to the things you can observe. You should certainly begin by becoming familiar with the names and locations of the brighter stars so that you can recognize them. Then you will find it easy to recognize a planet, for, whenever you observe a bright object where there should be no bright star, you will know that it must be a planet.

It is surprising how many people are not aware that the stars rise and set, how many are amazed that the stars move. These are things you can see simply by watching the sky for about an hour on some clear night. You cannot fail to see some stars rise, some set, and all of the stars change their positions toward the west. As a matter of fact, if you make careful observations of the movements of the stars by watching them for awhile every night for some time, you can learn a good deal about them. Toward the north, you will be watching stars that never rise or set. These stars move around the sky in counterclockwise circles with the North Star near the center.

Most of the motion you see in the skies at night is caused by the earth's motion in space. The circling of the stars in the north and the rising and setting of the others result from the rotation of the earth. The earth spins around from west to east, so the stars appear to move the opposite way. If you note which stars you see each night and in what part of the sky they have their position from night to night, you will see the effect of another motion of the earth upon the sky picture.

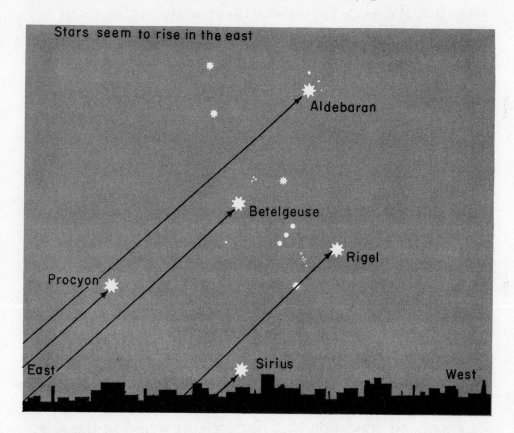

In the course of a year, the earth revolves once around the sun. Thus we see different stars at different seasons. All of the stars you can see tonight will be just a little west of their present positions tomorrow night at the same time. They will be a little further west on the next night, and so on. If you look at them once a week at the same hour of the night, you will see that the stars and constellations "march" slowly westward as our planet, earth, revolves eastward around the sun.

Your observations of motion in the nighttime sky need not end with the stars. Don't forget the moon and the planets. By watching where the full moon rises and sets and how high it gets, and noting the time of these events, you will see that when full, the moon moves exactly opposite to the sun.

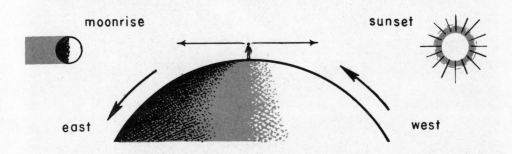

So far, we have mentioned only some of the things you can observe just by going out and looking at the sky with your eyes and without any other aid. In the next chapter, you will see that there are a great many more things you can observe in the sky if you use a few simple tools, similar to those that astronomers use. The real secret in understanding astronomy, whether you use the tools of an astronomer or not, is to go outdoors and look. Today you still can find the same entertainment and education that the ancients found in the skies, just by doing as they did. Observe the sky and remember what you see there.

Make a record of the things you see. Let it be your practice to keep a small notebook in which you write down the things you observe, whether with special tools or simply by looking. Record the date, time, and place of your observation, and all the other facts that you noted. It is fun to go over your record every now and then and read about the things you observed.

4 Tools to Help You Learn About the Sky

If you wish to learn more about the sky than you can by just looking at it with your unaided eyes, you can use several kinds of tools. Maps and charts are aids to learning the stars and constellations. Telescopes and binoculars help you see things that are faint or small. Sextants and theodolites are used to measure accurately the location of things. There are observatories and planetariums to visit where you learn from the work of professional astronomers. You should become familiar with all of these things, if you wish to have some real adventures with stars.

You may know the names of the stars and constellations, but can you recognize them in the sky? You must have a way of finding out where they are. Star maps show the locations of the stars just as earth maps show where cities and rivers and countries are. Star maps give you a picture of all of the stars in the sky just as they are arranged in the sky itself. Dots, circles, or star-like figures on a star map represent stars of different brightness. These maps give you the names used for the stars. They have lines to show how the stars are grouped into constellations and they give the names of the constellations. Usually, however, they show only the brighter stars and the outstanding constellations.

A star finder is a round map of the stars mounted inside of a holder. The star map can be turned around inside the holder which has a large opening in it. You can see only the part of the map under the opening. A calendar is printed around the edge of the holder. When you match the correct date on the map with the correct time on the holder, the stars you can see in the opening will be the same as the stars you can see in the sky at that time and date.

After you have learned the names of some stars and how to use a star finder, you may wish to find the exact position of some stars in the sky. You may even wish to use them the way navigators do, to check the latitude where you live. Astronomers, navigators, and engineers must observe star positions accurately for many reasons: to determine accurate time, to find a position on earth, or to measure the direction of a road or a bridge. If you wish to make similar use of the stars, you must learn how the sky is measured and what kind of tools astronomers and others use for making the measurements.

Of course, you have seen a map or globe of the earth and noticed the lines going across it. Maps and globes of the sky are divided up by lines just the way the others are. On the earth maps you can see dots at the north and south poles, and you can also see lines drawn between the poles. These lines called *meridians* are used for measuring *longitude.* You can find other lines like the equator drawn around the earth. These lines called *parallels* are used to measure *latitude.* The latitude of a city is its distance north and south of the equator. The longitude of a city is its distance east or west of Greenwich, a city in England.

The sky also has latitude and longitude. A sky map or globe has its north and south poles, a sky equator, lines between the poles in the sky, and other lines drawn around the sky parallel to its equator. These lines, like latitude and longitude, but called by different names, are used to measure the positions of the stars. The distance like latitude from the equator in the sky to a star is called the star's *declination*. The distance around the sky, like our longitude, is called the *hour angle* of a star.

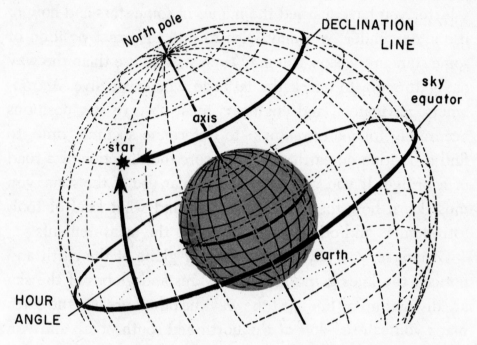

You do not have to measure the declination and hour angle for stars you want to study. Astronomers have measured these positions for all the important stars. They are given in books called almanacs. *The Nautical Almanac* and *The Air Almanac* give these positions for the stars which are used by sea and air navigators. Here are some examples:

Positions of the Brightest Stars

Name of Star	Declination	Hour Angle	Name of Star	Declination	Hour Angle
Aldebaran	16°N	292°	Regulus	12°N	208°
Rigel	8°S	282°	Spica	11°S	159°
Capella	46°N·	282°	Arcturus	19°N	147°
Betelguese	7°N	272°	Antares	26°S	113°
Sirius	17°S	259°	Vega	39°N	81°
Procyon	5°N	246°	Altair	9°N	63°
Pollux	28°N	244°	Deneb	45°N	50°

Star positions are also measured in another way without a star map. You find some bright star and all you do is measure two angles. These are called the angles of *altitude* and *azimuth*. Altitude is the height of a sky object measured in degrees from the horizon upward. It is zero degrees for a star which is exactly on the horizon, and 90 degrees (or one-fourth of a circle) for stars overhead. Azimuth is the position of a sky object measured horizontally in degrees starting from the North. For a star which is exactly north, azimuth is zero. It is 90 degrees for a star which is exactly east, 270 degrees when it is exactly west, and the circle is completed back to 360 degrees at north, where it becomes zero again. The altitude and azimuth of a

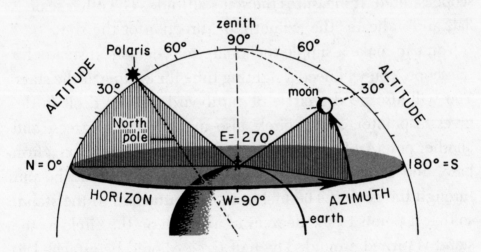

star locate its position exactly as you see it in the sky. The way in which its altitude and azimuth change is an exact record of the movement of a star. These are the angles that navigators measure when they observe star positions. They are also the angles you can measure and record to keep track of a star's movement. You can follow the movement of the sun, moon and planets too, in the same way.

The instrument you need to measure altitude and azimuth is an angle-measuring tool. Navigators use the kind which is called a sextant. This kind is held in your hand, and you use it by sighting both the horizon and the star at the same time. The reading scale then tells you the angle between the horizon and the star.

A sextant can be used only when there is a clear horizon to measure from, like the horizon at sea. On the land, where there are buildings, trees, or hills in the way, another instrument, the kind that engineers use, can serve the purpose. It is called a *theodolite*. A theodolite has a telescope which is pointed at the star, and two reading scales. One scale moves as the telescope is tilted. It measures the star's altitude. The other scale is flat, and indicates the azimuth, or direction of the star.

You can make a simple theodolite for yourself. Instead of a telescope, you will need a sighting tube for looking at the stars. You will also need a circle of cardboard measured off in degrees, a pointer, a half circle also measured in degrees, and another pointer. The whole circle should be mounted on a firm base, and a stand that can be turned around should be put through the center. The first pointer is attached to the stand, so that it points to the degrees of azimuth on the circle as the stand is turned around. The half circle should be attached to the sighting tube. Then the tube is attached to the top of the stand so that it can be tilted up and down. The second pointer should be fastened at the center of the half circle, so that it always points downward no matter how the sighting tube is tilted. This pointer will show the altitude of a star in degrees on the half circle when you aim the sighting tube at the star.

This kind of simple theodolite (also called a "Starscope")

will help you observe the stars and their motions. You can use it for the moon and the planets too. You should *never* observe the sun unless you protect your eyes. A piece of heavily exposed picture film, or a very heavily smoked glass will help protect your eyes, but extreme care must be taken to avoid getting the brilliant rays of the sun directly into your eyes. To do so might make you blind.

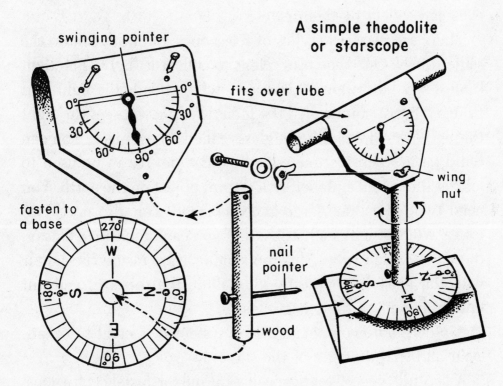

A simple theodolite or starscope

There are plenty of things to measure and observe about the moon, planets, and stars. You can start by finding the altitude of the North Star, which is always very nearly the same as your latitude. Try it. The angle you measure from the horizon to the North Star should be within a degree of the correct latitude of the place from which you are observing. Any map atlas will give you latitudes.

The next tool you may wish to try in getting to know the stars better is a telescope. Telescopes allow you to see more. First of all, they magnify things, making them appear larger. Thus you see them better. Second, they permit you to see as separated things two objects which are so close together that they look like one to your eyes alone. Third, they allow you to see very faint objects because they collect more light than your eyes can collect by themselves.

There are two basic types of telescopes, but both can do the same things. One type uses a lens to collect its light. The light from a star falls upon a glass lens, which bends the light and brings it into a point called the focus. The viewer sees this light through a small magnifying glass, called an eyepiece. You can build an inexpensive telescope of this type. It can be used to look at the moon, a planet, or a distant object on the earth. You need two lenses, one large and one small. You also need two tubes, which are of such a size that you can mount one lens on the end of each tube. Slip the smaller tube inside the larger with the lenses at opposite ends. Slide the tubes in and out until you can see the object clearly.

A much more complicated lens system is needed to obtain clear and sharp images of the stars.

A second type of telescope uses a mirror instead of a lens. The light of a star is allowed to fall on the surface of a curved mirror. The mirror reflects it, but in a slightly different direction, again concentrating all of the light at a point, called the focus, in front of the mirror. The observer uses his eyepiece magnifier to examine the light at this focus. He sees a brighter, sharper, and perhaps larger, image of the object.

If you wish to buy a complete telescope, keep several things in mind. For the same amount of money, you can buy a better reflecting telescope than a lens-type telescope. Do not pay too much attention to things like "power" in advertisements. The important thing is the size and quality of the mirror and lenses. The telescope mounting is important also. The legs of the mount should be firm and steady, so that the telescope will not

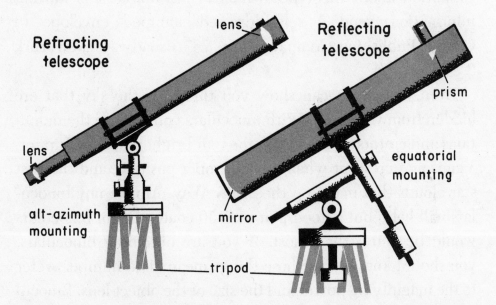

shake in the wind or when you touch it to make a slight adjustment. It is worth a little more money to pay for a better mounting. There are two types of mounting you might consider. One is called an alt-azimuth. It allows you to move the telescope up and down or around the horizon. The other is called an equatorial mount. It allows you to set the telescope to the viewing position of an object and then to follow it easily as it moves westward across the sky. Remember the stars seem to move because the earth is moving. An equatorial mounts lets your telescope move in the opposite direction to the earth's rotation.

A beginner should not purchase an expensive telescope. If your interest grows, you can sell it and buy a better one. A first telescope might well be a three- or four-inch reflecting telescope with an equatorial mounting, view finder, and three eyepieces. These can be bought at prices between $40.00 and $100.00. Before buying a telescope, you may wish to get information about the types which are available. For further information, send a self-addressed stamped envelope to Capitol Publishing Company, Inc., 737 Broadway, New York 3, New York.

Even binoculars can show you things in the sky that are hidden from your eyes. With binoculars you can see the mountains and craters on the moon, the four bright moons of Jupiter, Venus as a crescent when it is in proper position, and the vast star clouds that make up the Milky Way. Almost any binoculars will help, but a good pair of 7x50 coated prism binoculars would be better than most. If you are obtaining binoculars, you should know what these things mean. The numbers refer to the magnifying power and the size of the object lens. Binoculars described as 7x50 are 7 power and have lenses which are 50 millimeters across (about 2 inches). A smaller magnifying power will not make objects appear so large. Smaller lenses will not collect so much light and the objects seen with them will not be so bright. Coating helps to prevent light from reflecting away from the surfaces of the lenses. Coated binoculars transmit more light through the lenses and so give brighter images.

Besides those tools which you can buy, build, and use yourself, you can also learn a great deal more about astronomy from the professional astronomers, at observatories and planetariums. An observatory is a place where astronomers live and work, and where their laboratories are located.

Many of the observatories in the United States allow visitors to inspect their telescopes and domes. Some even permit visitors to look through the telescopes, while others conduct regular tours and lectures for visitors. The following is a list of some of the best known observatories in our country. If you live near some, or travel nearby on your vacation, you might write or call to find out about their programs for visitors:

Some of the Largest Observatories in the United States

Lowell Observatory
  Flagstaff, Ariz.

Lick Observatory
  Mt. Hamilton, Calif.

Mount Palomar Observatory
  Mount Palomar, Calif.

Mount Wilson Observatory
  Mount Wilson, Calif.

High Altitude Observatory
  Climax, Colorado

U.S. Naval Observatory
  Washington, D. C.

Dearborn Observatory
  Evanston, Ill.

Goethe Link Observatory
  Brooklyn, Indiana

Harvard College Observatory
  Cambridge, Mass.

Observatory of the Univ. of Michigan
  Ann Arbor

McMath-Hulbert Observatory
  Lake Angelus, Mich.

Princeton Observatory
  Princeton, N. J.

Sacramento Peak Observatory
  Sunspot, New Mexico

Rutherfurd Observatory
  New York, N. Y.

Perkins Observatory
  Delaware, Ohio

Sproul Observatory
  Swarthmore, Pa.

McDonald Observatory
  Mount Locke, Texas

Leander McCormick Observatory
  Charlottesville, Va.

Yerkes Observatory
  Williams Bay, Wisconsin

If you do manage to visit an observatory, you may be somewhat surprised at the equipment you will see. You may see long slender tubes, like the 40-inch telescope at the Yerkes Observatory, largest in the world. Or they may be huge open frames with mirrors at the bottom, like the great 100-inch telescope at Mount Wilson and 200-inch telescope at Palomar. All sorts of complicated instruments may be mounted on them, for taking photographs, for recording the strength of light, or for measuring temperature at great distances. Their domes will be cold in winter and hot in summer, the same as outside, to prevent currents of air from spoiling the view.

The astronomers themselves may be busy in guiding the instruments, changing the photographic plates, reading meters

Mt. Wilson-Palomar Observatories — 200-inch Hale telescope dome with shutter open

or adjusting recording devices. Do not expect to see a large number of men busily engaged in peering patiently through telescopes. Many modern astronomers never look through telescopes in their work. They may be off in a laboratory somewhere working at a computing machine, examining photographs with measuring machines, or preparing tables and notes of their work. At a radio observatory, of course no one can *look* at anything through the telescope. A radio telescope may be shaped like a huge bowl or it may be a set of wires strung out on poles. The observing is done automatically in most cases, and the facts read from charts or graphs, and photographs of meter readings.

A Planetarium is another place you can go to learn about the

Planetarium Projector, Haydn Planetarium

stars. A Planetarium has special equipment just to teach people about the sky. The heart of a Planetarium is a giant instrument mounted in the center of a bowl-shaped room. It is a very complex piece of machinery designed to show how the skies look from anywhere on earth at any time of the day or night in any year. The sun, moon, stars, and planets can be moved in a man-made sky to show you what they look like and how they behave in the real sky. Many cleverly-made devices are also used to show you other things, like an eclipse of the sun or moon, the Northern Lights, a shower of "shooting stars," or to take you on an imaginary trip to the moon or a distant planet.

There are ten large Planetariums in the United States. Their hours and programs are quite varied so that, before planning a visit to one, you should write or call for its schedule. There are also over one hundred small Planetariums in schools, colleges, and small museums throughout the country. Their programs are less extensive, because their equipment is simpler and their staffs are smaller.

These Are the Cities Which Have Large Planetariums
That You Can Visit

New York, N. Y..........................The American Museum-Hayden Planetarium
81st St. at Central Park West, N. Y. 24, N. Y.

Chapel Hill, N. C. ....The Morehead Planetarium
University of North Carolina, Chapel Hill, N. C.

Chicago, Ill. ....The Adler Planetarium
900 E. Achsah Bond Dr., Chicago 5, Ill.

Colorado Springs, Colo. ...........U.S. Air Force Academy Planetarium
Colorado Springs, Colo.

Boston, Mass. ....The Hayden Planetarium
Science Park, Museum of Science, Boston, Mass.

Los Angeles, Calif. ....Griffith Observatory and Planetarium
Griffith Park, Los Angeles 27, Calif.

San Francisco, Calif. ....The Morrison Planetarium
California Academy of Sciences, Golden Gate Park,
San Francisco 18, Calif.

Flint, Mich. ....The Longway Planetarium
Flint Junior College and Community Science
Center, Flint, Mich.

Philadelphia, Pa. ....The Fels Planetarium
The Franklin Institute, 20th St. at
Benjamin Franklin Parkway, Philadelphia 3, Pa.

Pittsburgh, Pa. ....Buhl Planetarium & Institute of Popular Science
Federal & W. Ohio Sts., Pittsburgh 12, Pa.

5 The Moon—Our Nearest Neighbor in Space

Have you ever seen the moon in the daytime? Have you ever wondered what happens to the moon when you cannot see it in the sky? What is the moon? How does it affect us?

The moon is the earth's nearest neighbor in space. It is a large object about a quarter of a million miles away from the earth. Although it measures 2,160 miles across through the center, it is only about one-fourth of the earth's diameter. Like the earth, it is solid, but it has no air or water. Except for the sun, it is the most important object in the sky so far as we are concerned. It gave us the unit called the month in our calendar. It often lights the night-time and it is the most important cause of the tides in the earth's oceans.

Some night when you can see the moon clearly, notice and try to remember the location of some of the brighter stars that are near it. To help your memory, draw a sketch of the position of the moon and the stars around it. Label with their names the stars you know. Those you do not know you can find on a star map. Then look at the moon again at the same hour on the next night and notice its location compared to the same stars. Draw a new sketch of the moon's position. Compare the two pictures you have drawn. Now what can you tell about the location of the moon on two successive nights?

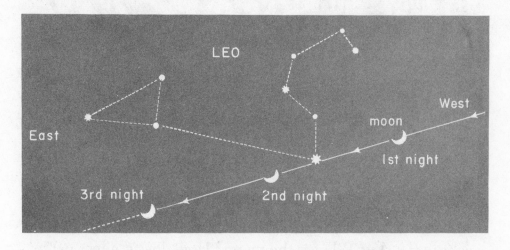

You should be able to observe that on the second night the moon seemed to be east of its location on the first night. And if you were to do the same thing for several more nights, you would see that the moon will change its position the same amount each night, always moving toward the east.

Since the earth is spinning around on its axis once each day, the moon must rise and set once a day, just like the sun, the stars and the planets. It rises in the east and sets somewhere in the west. But the moon is also traveling around the earth, in an eastward direction. It takes 27⅓ days to go once around the earth. For this reason it appears to be a little farther east in the sky day after day. This also explains why the moon seems to require more time to rise and set than the sun and stars.

Facing south, find some convenient landmark which you can watch each night from your home. On the night the moon is over this landmark, note the exact time. The next night observe the time when the moon appears over the same landmark. How long did it take the moon to go completely around the sky? Was it just 24 hours, or was it longer than one day? If you make your observations carefully, you will see that the trip takes about 24 hours and 50 minutes. Here is the reason.

On the first night, when you saw the moon over the landmark, you were looking into a certain position in space. On the next night, the moon was east of that position in space when it returned over the landmark. The moon had moved a certain distance eastward around the earth during the day, so it took the moon nearly an extra hour or almost 25 hours to return to your landmark.

THE PHASES OF THE MOON

Everybody notices how the moon's shape and appearance change as it goes around the earth. This goes on slowly every day taking about four weeks to complete a cycle which then begins all over again. These changes are known as the phases of the moon. They take place because the moon goes around the earth and because we see different amounts of sunlight reflected from it.

The bright side of the moon is the half facing the sun. Once every four weeks, the moon comes almost directly between the earth and the sun. At that time, the bright side of the moon is turned away from the earth. This is known as the new moon phase and at this time we cannot see it. A few days after the new moon, the moon has moved so that we see a bit of the sunlit side. It then appears as a crescent moon in the sky, with its horns, or tips, pointing away from the sun.

One week after the new moon, the moon has moved about a quarter of the way around the earth and we can see half of its bright surface. This is known as the first quarter moon.

About two weeks after the moon was new, it has moved halfway around the earth to a point almost opposite the sun. This is the beautiful full moon. Then we see the whole lighted face of the moon. It faces the night side of the earth, and you see a fully round, lighted moon.

On the nights after the full moon phase the sunlit surface begins to turn away from the earth. It is waning at this time, which means that it is growing smaller. In a week, again only half of the lighted surface can be seen, and the moon is at its third and last quarter phase. For another week after that, continuing to wane, the part of the moon we can see becomes

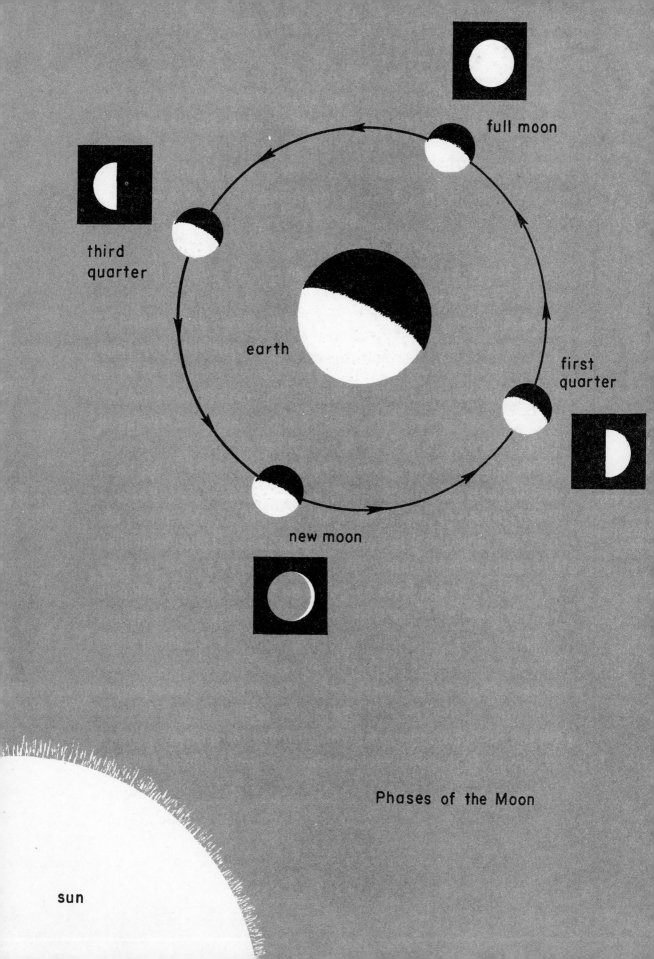

full moon

third
quarter

earth

first
quarter

new moon

Phases of the Moon

sun

smaller and smaller. It begins to look like a crescent and soon becomes a new moon again. When it reaches this position between the earth and the sun, none of its bright face is visible. Then a new cycle of the moon's phases starts.

Count the number of days on the calendar from one new moon to the next. You should find that there are about 29 or 30. But do you remember how long it takes the moon to go around the earth? It was $27\frac{1}{3}$ days, not $29\frac{1}{2}$. The moon takes longer to go through its phases than it takes to go around the earth. That is because the phases are caused by sunlight, and the earth is moving around the sun a certain distance during the time the moon is going around the earth. To go through its complete cycle of phases, the moon has to travel a little more than just one trip around the earth. It takes about $29\frac{1}{2}$ days to do this.

Have you ever noticed how large the moon appears when it rises or sets? Does it seem to look smaller when it is high in the sky? That is a very strange thing, which scientists have never fully explained. Actually, the moon is not larger when it rises, it just appears to be. It also may look a little red or orange when it is low in the sky. This happens because red light passes more easily than blue light through the thicker layers of air close to the earth's surface. The reddish color of the sun at dusk and dawn is caused in the same way.

THE TIDES

It will be easy for you to see that the tides are caused mostly by the moon. If you have the chance to visit a beach, or some other part of the coast, check the time of high tide each day for several days in a row. Or, if you cannot visit the beach or sea coast, look up the tide table in a newspaper. Either way you will find out how long it takes from high tide on one day to the same high tide on the day following. It should be about 24 hours and 50 minutes. Where have you seen that figure before? It is the same time that the moon takes to appear in the same part of the sky as it did the day before. This shows you the direct relation of the moon to the tides.

If you live anywhere near an ocean, or if you ever visit ocean beaches, no doubt you are familiar with the tides. The waters of the oceans rise and fall regularly each day. In most places, they are highest twice a day and lowest twice a day.

The moon causes the waters of the oceans to rise in places on earth beneath it. But the waters also rise on the opposite side of the earth. These two tides are the high tides that come twice a day. At other places on earth, between these high tides, the waters are lower than normal and low tides are taking place.

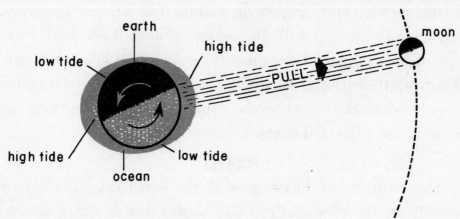

To understand what causes two high and two low tides per day, you might think of them as they are shown in the illustration. The pull of the moon upon the earth is not the same on all parts of the earth because the earth is round. Therefore some parts of the earth are closer to the moon than others. The result, shown in the picture, is that the waters of the oceans rise on the side closest to the moon and also on the side farthest from the moon. The sun also causes tides but they are not as great as the moon's tides because the sun is so much farther away.

The tides at new moon and at full moon are of special interest. On these days, since the earth, moon, and sun are almost exactly in line, the tides of the moon and of the sun occur in the same direction and at the same time. As a result, the high tides are higher and the low tides are lower. These are called spring tides, but they come about twice every month and not just in the spring. At other times, when the moon is in any other phase, the tides of the moon and of the sun occur at different hours, and they tend to make each other smaller.

If you visit the beaches in the summer, your knowledge of the tides and of the moon's phases should help in several ways. Remember to expect higher than usual tides on the days when the moon is new or full. Remember also that the high tides come about an hour (more nearly 50 minutes) later each day. Knowing these things may help you avoid getting your beach towel and lunch soaked by the rising tide by leaving them too close to the edge of the water.

ECLIPSES

The path of the moon around the earth does not follow exactly on the same path as the earth takes in going around the sun. The moon's orbit is slightly inclined to the line between the earth and sun. Thus, the new moon usually does not come directly between the earth and sun. But sometimes it does cross directly between them. Then it causes an eclipse of the *sun* to take place.

An eclipse of the *moon* occurs at times when the moon is full. The earth is a solid object and it has a shadow—a long, cone-shaped shadow extending about 860,000 miles into space. Since the moon is never that far from the earth, it cannot pass beyond the shadow. But, because its path around the earth is slightly inclined, it can pass above or below the shadow. This is what it does most of the time. Once in a while, however, the path of the moon takes it right through the shadow of the earth. When that happens an eclipse of the moon takes place. Since the moon is opposite to the sun at such times, it is the full moon which becomes eclipsed.

Photograph of Lunar Eclipse showing the moon at five minute intervals

From the time it first enters the earth's shadow, an hour may pass before the moon is completely darkened. Most of the time it remains dimly visible throughout the whole eclipse. As it enters the shadow of the earth, a dark curve begins to appear on the eastern side of the moon. The dark curve gradually covers more and more of the brightness of the full moon, until the moon is dimmed completely. But the shadow is not black. It appears as a very dark red, like the color of copper. The redness is from these rays in sunlight which have been bent around the earth by the earth's atmosphere.

Although eclipses of the moon do not occur as often as eclipses of the sun, you may have a chance to see them more often. Every time the moon is eclipsed, the whole night-time side of the earth can view the event.

Dates of Total Lunar Eclipses Which Will Be Visible From the United States

March 13, 1960	Visible throughout the United States
Sept. 5, 1960	In central and western United States, only the beginning in the eastern part.
Aug. 25, 1962	Throughout the United States
Dec. 31, 1963	In western United States
June 24, 1964	In the eastern part of the United States
Dec. 18, 1964	Visible throughout the United States

THE SURFACE OF THE MOON

The moon is one of the favored objects in the sky for owners of small telescopes. Even a small pair of binoculars, will show you many wonderful features of the face of the moon. Its surface contains great mountain ranges, huge flat plains, thousands of craters, and systems of rays stretching hundreds of miles across its surface. You can see some of these features without a telescope or binoculars because they are so large. Together they make up the face of what we call the "man in the moon."

The eyes, nose, and mouth of the "man" are caused by the "maria," a Latin word which means "seas." Years ago people thought that they were oceans and seas, because they look dark. We know now that they are really flat plains which appear dark because they do not reflect sunlight too well.

Northern portion of the moon at last quarter

Other parts of the moon are much brighter because they are much more rough or rugged. If you can examine the moon with binoculars or with a telescope, you will be able to see some of the craters, because they are quite large. The largest, Clavius,

61

is about 200 miles in diameter, and there are many 30 miles or more across. The best time to see the mountains and craters on the moon is not when the moon is full. Everything is too bright then, and hard to see because no shadows are visible. When the moon is at first quarter or last quarter, or even when it is a crescent, you can see things much better. At such times, the high objects on the moon cast shadows, and their details can be seen in relief against the dark shadows.

The first visitors to the moon will find a strange place, in spite of how much they learned by studying it from the earth. If they want to spend a day on the moon, they will have to plan their trip to last for a whole month. A day on the moon lasts for $27\frac{1}{3}$ earth days. Since the moon has no air, water, or food, they will have to carry along all they would need for the journey and for the return trip to the earth. The moon's sky will always be clear and cloudless; its surface will be blazing hot and brilliant by day, but bitterly cold by night.

If you could spend a day on the moon, it would begin with the strangest sunrise you had ever seen. There would be no dawn, no warning glow. In an instant, the sun would be above the horizon. Without air to shield them, the rocks and crater walls around you would heat up rapidly and reflect sunlight in a dazzling way. The temperature would rise to the boiling point of water, or even higher. You would have to find some shelter immediately, to shield yourself from the burning sunlight.

The day would last for about two weeks of earth time. During this day, the sky would remain as dark as though it were night, and it would be possible to see stars shining in all parts of the sky right up to the edge of the sun. The sun and stars would drift gradually across the sky as the moon rotated beneath them.

At the end of the moon day, the sun would set rapidly and the surface of the moon would grow dark in an instant. However, there would be some light remaining even after the sun went down. This is earthlight, shining from the earth onto the surface of the moon. This is the same earthlight we sometimes see on the moon when we observe "the old moon in the new moon's arms." The sky would remain dark, and the stars would

Surface of moon with earth in the distance

shine brilliantly and steadily, without twinkling as they do when seen from earth.

With the setting of the sun, the rocks and craters of the moon begin to cool rapidly, losing the heat of the day into space. There is no air to serve as a blanket to keep it in. Within hours, the temperature of the moon's surface would drop to freezing, and then below, down to perhaps 250 degrees below zero, Fahrenheit. During this time, you would have to find some way to keep warm. The night also would remain for two more weeks, the longest, coldest, bleakest night you had ever experienced. Finally, the sun would rise for another day two weeks long.

If you traveled around the moon, you might have two experiences that no man has ever enjoyed. For one thing, you would find walking, jumping, and running, even with an awkward space suit, much easier than they are on earth. So much easier, in fact, that you would probably have to learn to do them all over again. Since the moon is so much smaller and lighter than the earth, you would weigh only one-sixth of what you weigh on earth. The equipment you had to carry would weigh one-sixth as well. But your muscles would be the same, of course, so you would have to learn how to use them all over again with less weight to control them.

The other experience would be one that men have been looking forward to for a long time, a chance to visit the other side of the moon and to discover the cause of the craters and rays. Because the same side of the moon always faces the earth, no one has ever seen the other side of the moon. Some say, without much authority, that it might be quite different from the side we always see. But this is not very likely. Because the moon moves in an irregular way, we can see, at one time or another, almost six-tenths of its surface. As we look a little around the moon's edge at the times when it is possible, we observe that it appears the same as the part we always can see. The other side, the part we have never seen, probably also has mountains, valleys, rocks, plains, and craters.

Of all the things we see in the sky, the most familiar is the sun. How well should you know something that you see every day? See how well you know the sun. Are the following statements about it TRUE or FALSE?

- The sun is nearest to the earth in July, when our weather is hottest.
- The sun always rises in the east and sets in the west.
- You will see the sun overhead at noon tomorrow.
- The sun is solid inside, like the earth.
- The light and heat from the sun is produced by the burning of the sun's material.
- Spots on the sun are storms.
- No more than one eclipse of the sun can occur in a year, and it is usually several years between eclipses.

It may surprise you to learn that *all* of the above statements are False! If you didn't get all of them right, do not be disappointed; few people would. Try them on your friends.

Of course, if you do this, people will expect you to be able to show why your answer is correct. For example, how would you show the difference between the summer and winter positions of the sun?

The earth is nearest to the sun in the winter, when the weather is coldest in January. We like to say the distance from the earth to the sun is 93,000,000 miles, but this is its *average* distance. The earth travels around the sun in a path called an ellipse. An ellipse is an oval-shaped curve. Sometimes an ellipse is long and cigar-shaped. Sometimes it is almost as round as a circle.

You can draw a circle easily. Place a thumb tack near the center of a piece of cardboard. Then get a piece of string about 8 inches long and tie both ends to the tack. Put the point of a pencil in the loop of the string and, holding the string tight, swing it around. The line you draw on the cardboard is a circle if you continue it until you come around to the point where you started.

If the earth travelled around the sun in a circle, we would always be the same distance away from the sun. But astronomers observe that we are not. In July, the earth is about 94,500,000 miles from the sun, and in January we are about 91,500,000 miles from it. Measure the distance of two points on opposite sides of your circle and you will see they are the same distance from the center where the tack is. The earth cannot be travelling in a circle since its distance from the sun changes. Its path is an ellipse.

Now let's try drawing an ellipse. This time, draw a one inch line near the center of a piece of cardboard. Place a thumb tack at each end of the line. Tie one end of the 8-inch string to each tack. Again place the point of a pencil in the loop of the string and swing it around, holding the string tight. Continue drawing a line around the two tacks until you return to the point where you started. Help the string over the thumb tacks when it crosses them. Now you have drawn an ellipse. Each one of the thumb tacks is at one focus of the ellipse. This is the kind of path or orbit the earth has as it travels around the sun.

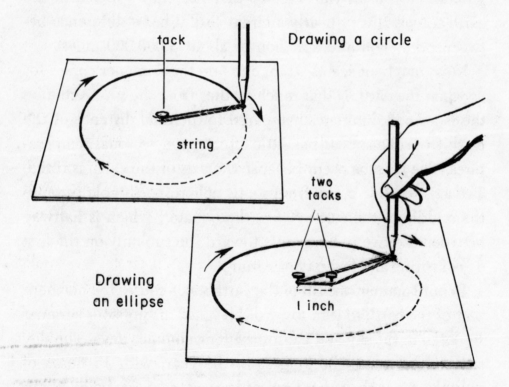

Drawing a circle

tack

string

two tacks

Drawing an ellipse

1 inch

The sun is located at one focus of the ellipse. Remove one of the tacks and let the other one represent the sun. Now see that the orbit comes closest to this tack at one point and the point opposite is farthest away. The earth is at this closest point with respect to the sun in January. Astronomers call that position of the earth perihelion (peh-ri-*heel*-yun). In July, the earth reaches the opposite, most distant position, called aphelion (ah-*feel*-yun).

The true orbit of the earth around the sun is not nearly as flat as the ellipse you have drawn. If you wanted to draw the earth's orbit in correct scale, you would have to use a piece of string 125 inches long, keeping the two tacks one inch apart. You might try drawing this kind of ellipse with chalk on the ground. If you do you will see that the ellipse in which the earth travels is very nearly a circle. Still it has a difference between perihelion and aphelion of about 3,000,000 miles.

Now, maybe it seems strange to you that summer comes for us when the earth is that much farther from the sun. Actually, this is a small difference compared to the total distance of the earth from the sun. It has little effect upon seasonal temperatures. The seasons occur because the axis of the earth is tilted. The axis is a line going from south pole to north pole through the middle of the earth. Thus, the equator, which is halfway between the two poles, points toward the sun only on the first day of spring and first day of autumn.

In our summer, the tilt of the earth's axis causes the northern part of the earth to lean toward the sun. This puts our summer sun high in the sky and causes the long summer days. The day summer begins is the longest in the year, with 15 hours of sunlight. Since the sun is high and spends so many hours in our sky, summer is a warm season.

Notice where the earth is when we have winter. The earth's axis is still tilted the same way, but now it causes the northern part of the world to lean away from the sun. As a result, the sun is low in our sky and on the first day of winter it spends only 8 hours of the day above the horizon. We, in the Northern

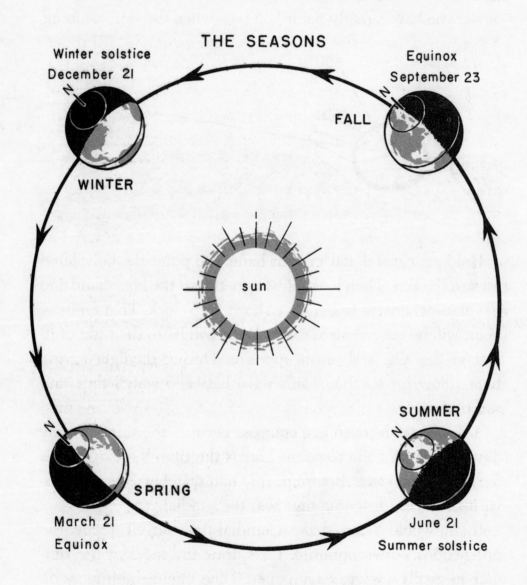

THE SEASONS

Winter solstice
December 21

WINTER

Equinox
September 23

FALL

sun

SPRING

March 21
Equinox

SUMMER

June 21
Summer solstice

Hemisphere, do not get as much heat from this low winter sun which spends so little time in the sky. Thus winter is a cold season.

69

One thing you will surely notice from observing the sun and following its path in the sky is that it is always located in the south at noontime. This can give you a very valuable way of finding direction. If you have any kind of a watch or clock along, you have a ready-made compass when the sun is shining.

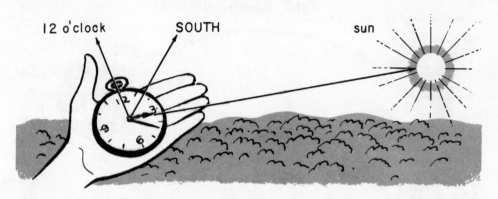

Hold your watch flat in your hand and point the hour hand toward the sun. Then look midway between the hour hand and the place where the watch face shows 12 o'clock. That midway point will be very close to south. West will be to the right of it, east to the left, and north opposite. During daylight saving time, allow for the hour difference between watch time and sun time.

A watch can be used as a compass because the sun takes one day to go from noon to noon. This is the time the earth takes to spin around once. Before people had watches, a very popular instrument for telling time was the sundial.

If you would like to make a sundial for yourself, follow the instructions shown opposite. First draw the faces of the sundial on cardboard or heavy paper. Then mount both faces on a piece of wood, matching them carefully. This kind of dial should be mounted so that the pin or dowel going through the center always points toward the North Star and the 12 o'clock marking on both faces points toward north. The wooden board on which the dial faces are mounted should make an angle with

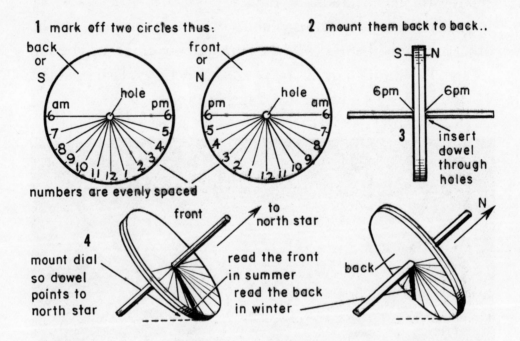

1 mark off two circles thus:

back or S

am 6 7 8 9 10 11 12 1 2 3 4 5 pm 6

hole

numbers are evenly spaced

front or N

pm 6 5 4 3 2 1 12 11 10 9 am 6

hole

2 mount them back to back..

S — N

6pm   6pm

3 insert dowel through holes

4 mount dial so dowel points to north star

front

to north star

read the front in summer
read the back in winter

back

N

the ground which depends on latitude. This angle will be exactly right if the pin or dowel points to the north star.

SUNSPOTS

Sometimes the whole surface of the sun appears to be covered with millions of tiny bright spots, surrounded by little rivers of darkness. These bright spots, each several hundred miles in size, change their appearance constantly. Each lasts only for a few minutes. They are called *granules*.

We can also see many dark areas at certain times. They are called sunspots. They come and go, lasting anywhere from a few days to several months. They drift across the sun's face, showing us that the sun is rotating, or spinning around. It rotates once in about 25 days in the center, where its equator is located. Farther away from its equator, near the poles, the sun rotates once in about 30 days.

There are certain times when hardly any sunspots can be observed, and other times when a great many are seen. The sun seems to go through cycles or periods of activity, lasting about 11 years. This is known as the sunspot cycle.

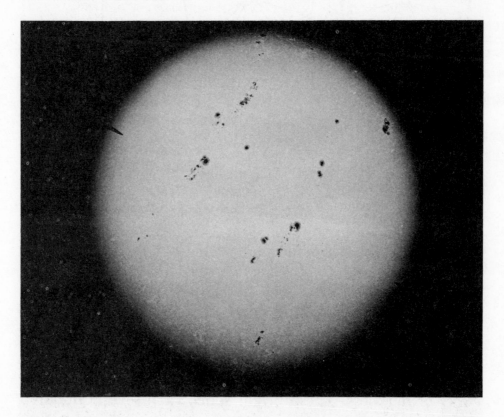

Sunspots

It is not correct to call sunspots "storms" on the sun, as many people do. They are quite different from storms on earth. Sunspots might be better described as cool spots, or quiet spots on the sun, for that seems to be what they are. The temperature in a sunspot is several thousand degrees cooler than in the surrounding bright face of the sun. The gases in a sunspot seem to be less active than in the surrounding areas.

There is another kind of solar activity which may be better described as a storm, though it too is not at all like any earth storm. During periods of increased sunspot activity, the sun also has a great many flares. These flares are regions where the sun grows quite active. Flares are hotter than the surrounding face of the sun. They give off more energy, more light, and have more effect upon the earth. When a large flare develops on the sun, radio communications may be disrupted for hours or even days. Even long distance telegraph messages may be

Aurora Borealis

blocked. And on the nights after a flare takes place, we may be able to see some of those brilliant displays of moving colored lights called the Northern Lights, or the Aurora Borealis.

73

ECLIPSES OF THE SUN

In the picture below, you can see parts of the sun which are above the bright surface we ordinarily see. The picture was taken during an eclipse of the sun. When the moon covers the sun during an eclipse, the sky grows dark, and we can see faint outer parts of the sun which are normally hidden by the brightness of day. Then we see the corona, the faint outer atmosphere

Total eclipse

of the sun, which extends outward for millions of miles. It glows with a faint, pearly-white light. We also see parts of the reddish chromosphere, a thin layer just above the sun's bright face. We can also see some of the sun's gases extending above it's surface, like great jets, or clouds, or arches of flame-like brilliance. These gaseous extensions are called prominences.

74

Total eclipses of the sun are not really rare events, since they occur almost every year. When one takes place, it can be seen from only a small part of the earth, the thin path along the earth where the shadow of the moon touches the surface. So in any one location, it is rare to see a total eclipse. If you wish to see one, you may have to travel many miles. It is well worth it, because a total eclipse is one of the most beautiful events you will ever see in the sky.

The sun may remain covered for only a few seconds, or for minutes. The longest possible eclipse of the sun lasts for only about 7½ minutes. After that, the moon moves off in its journey around the earth and the sun returns to normal in the daytime sky.

The next total eclipse of the sun in the United States will be in 1959, on October 2, and will be visible in the southeastern part of New England. After that, there will be another on March 7, 1970, visible in the central part of Florida. This one will also be seen in northern Mexico.

THE SUN'S ENERGY

Have you ever wondered what makes the stars shine, or where the light and heat of the sun come from? From what we know about the age of the earth—geologists tell us that it may be 5 billion years old—the sun has been shining for a long time. It appears that the sun has been sending out its light and heat into space all that time just as much as it does today. Can you imagine any fuel that would be able to supply so much energy for so long? Even if the sun were made of pure coal, it would have burned up completely in about 50 years at the rate it gives off energy.

From their studies of the sun and the stars, astronomers have learned that the sun's energy comes from atoms. The sun is an atomic machine, supplying light and heat by atomic reactions going on inside its hot interior. You have probably read about our efforts here on earth to obtain power from the atom. First there was the atom bomb, which released great energy very fast. Then we built atomic reactors, which slowed the process up and allowed the energy to be used for peaceful purposes. The atom bomb and the atomic reactors obtain their power by splitting large heavy atoms, using the method called fission. The sun makes its energy by an even better method called fusion.

Fusion is the kind of process that goes on in a hydrogen bomb. Hydrogen is the smallest atom, so it cannot be split. Instead, it can be combined with other hydrogen atoms to build up a new material, helium. It takes four hydrogen particles to make one helium particle. But the helium atom doesn't weigh quite as much as the hydrogen atoms that fused to make it. A little bit of the hydrogen material is lost by being converted directly into an enormous amount of energy. That is where the hydrogen bomb gets its terrifying power.

Scientists are now trying to slow down the process of fusion to obtain energy for peacetime uses. The scientists are having trouble doing this because the fusion of hydrogen particles into helium will only take place at very high temperatures like those in the interior of the sun. There the temperature is over 50 million degrees. The sun contains over 2,000, million, million, million, million tons of material, and 90% of it is hydrogen. This is the sun's fuel. The sun is an enormous fusion reactor.

Have you ever considered the many ways in which this

energy is used on earth? It warms the earth and lights the day. It also makes the rain, causes the winds to blow, and moves the currents in the waters of the earth. We owe a debt to the

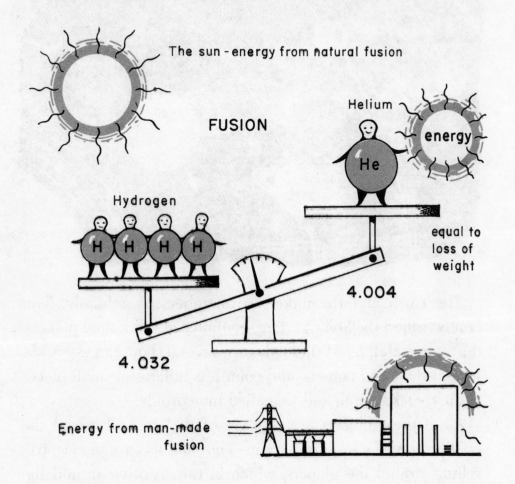

The sun - energy from natural fusion

FUSION

Helium

energy

He

Hydrogen

H H H H

equal to
loss of
weight

4.004

4.032

Energy from man-made
fusion

sun for the plants we use for food, and for the animals that live on the plants; for the lumber we obtain from our forests; and for the coal, oil, and gas we use for fuel and other things. It may not be long before you will see your home lighted, heated in winter, and cooled in the summer with power obtained directly from the sun or with power obtained by copying here on earth the same process that is going on inside of the sun and the stars.

7 Captives of the Sun

The earth and the moon are members of a family. This family, called the Solar System, contains one star, nine planets, thirty-one satellites of these planets, several thousand asteroids, several thousand comets, and countless billions of small pieces of dust, rock, metal, and ice called meteoroids.

All of these objects are captives of the sun. All except the satellites revolve around the sun. The satellites are moons, travelling around the planets, which in turn revolve around the sun. All are held in orbits by the enormous attraction of the sun. There is much more material in the sun than there is in all the rest of the solar system. This material has so much attraction that it holds captive objects ten billion miles or more away from the sun.

The main objects of the solar system, other than the sun, are the planets. The word planet comes from an ancient Greek word meaning wanderer. Since ancient times people have known that the planets move among the stars whereas the stars always stay in the same pattern in the sky picture. Five of the planets are close enough to the earth and bright enough to be seen without a telescope. When you have learned to recognize the planets, you will see why the ancients called them wanderers.

You can recognize the planets in several ways: by their location, by their brightness, and by their color. Any bright object in the sky located where no bright star is supposed to be should be suspected of being a planet. You can recognize planets because they usually do not twinkle as the stars do. They are so much closer to us than the stars that their light seems to be more steady.

Facts About the Planets, the Sun, and the Moon

Name of Planet	Distance from sun (millions of miles)	Period of revolution (length of year)	Period of Rotation (length of day)	Diameter in miles	What you would weigh if 100 lbs. on earth	Number of moons
Mercury	36	88 days	88 days	3,010	38 lbs.	0
Venus	67	225 days	30 days ?	7,610	88 lbs.	0
Earth	93	365¼ days	24 hours	7,918	100 lbs.	1
Mars	142	687 days	24h 37m	4,140	39 lbs.	2
Jupiter	483	11-9/10 yrs.	9h 50m	86,900	265 lbs.	12
Saturn	886	29½ yrs.	10h 2m	71,500	117 lbs.	9
Uranus	1783	84 years	10h 50m	29,500	105 lbs.	5
Neptune	2791	164¾ yrs.	15h 50m	26,800	123 lbs.	2
Pluto	3671	248½ yrs.	?	3,600?	16 lbs.?	?
The sun			24¾ days	864,000	279 lbs.	
The moon			27⅓ days	2,160	16 lbs.	

When you have recognized a planet, observe carefully its position among the stars on a map of the sky and note the date of your observation. Then look at the planet every night for a few weeks and mark its new positions on your map. You will notice that the planet, in changing its position, moves generally toward the east among the stars. This motion of the planets is caused by their revolution around the sun in an eastward direction.

You can observe something else about the planets and the moon. You can see them only in a certain part of the sky, never in any other part. You never can see any planet or the moon near the North Star, or in the Big Dipper, or among the stars of the Summer Triangle. All of the planets, including the earth, travel around the sun at almost the same level, or plane. When you look for the planets you will find them only within a narrow belt of the sky. This belt is called the Zodiac.

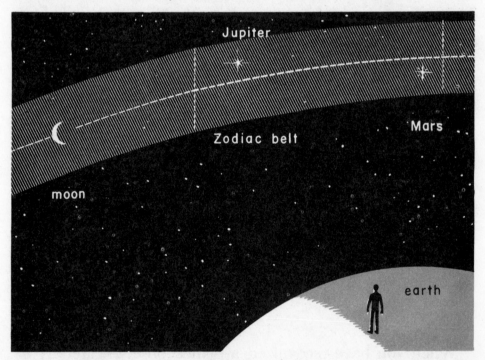

You will find it much easier to recognize the planets if you know something about each one. Let's take a quick trip through the Solar System to meet each of the planets.

Mercury is the smallest planet and the one closest to the sun. It travels around the sun very swiftly, at about 30 miles per second. It always keeps the same side of its surface turned toward the sun. It does this because it rotates once on its axis in the same length of time it takes to go around the sun. Thus, one side of Mercury is very hot like melted solder and the other side is very cold like dry ice. Mercury has no atmosphere and probably no water.

About once every four months, Mercury passes in between the sun and the earth and comes closest to the earth, about 57 million miles away.

Of the five visible planets, Mercury is the most difficult to observe. Since its position is so close to the sun, it is always seen close to the sun in the sky. It can be observed only at the time of sunset or sunrise, and then very briefly.

VENUS

Venus, the second planet out from the sun, is almost the twin of the earth in size. It is only a little smaller than our planet. It also comes closer to the earth than any other planet. It is within 26 million miles of us once every year and a half. In spite of its close approach, astronomers know less about Venus than they do about some planets much farther away.

There are two main reasons for this. First, when Venus comes closest to us it is between the sun and the earth. Then it is in a "new" phase and its bright side is turned away from us. When the bright side of Venus is turned toward us during the full phase, the planet is much further away from the earth. In its full phase, Venus appears smaller in the sky than when it is a thin crescent. Second, the surface of Venus has never been seen. The planet seems to be covered completely by a deep layer of clouds, so thick that we cannot see through them to the surface. Astronomers have observed faint markings at the top of the clouds which appear to be dust storms or dark clouds.

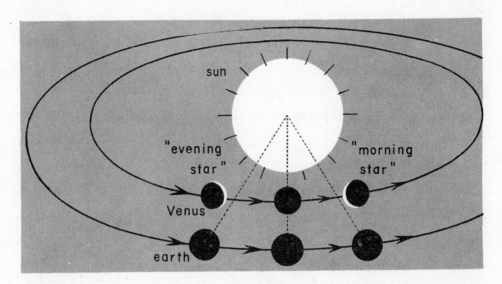

Do you ever remember seeing Venus as a brilliant evening star? It appeared as a bright object just after sunset, shining in the west or southwest, in the glow of the setting sun. It was the first bright object to be seen in the sky after the sun went down. It stayed there while the sky grew dark, and set shortly after night came. Did you wonder what became of it weeks later when it was no longer visible as an evening star? If you had gotten up early in the morning, you would have seen Venus again as a morning star, coming up above the horizon before the eastern sky grew bright, remaining as the glow of sunrise appeared, and finally fading into the dawn.

Venus becomes a morning and evening star about every year and a half. It is so brilliant at the times it appears thus that you cannot mistake it for any other sky object. It is brighter than anything else we see at night except the moon, brighter, too, than any star.

EARTH AND MARS

The third planet from the sun is, of course, the earth on which you live. It is about three times larger than Mercury, a bit larger than Venus, and the only planet we are sure has life on it. Beyond the earth the next planet outward from the sun is Mars. This planet is about half the size of the earth. Aside from the earth, it is the planet we know best because the views we get of it are so good. Have you ever noticed this bright, reddish object in the sky?

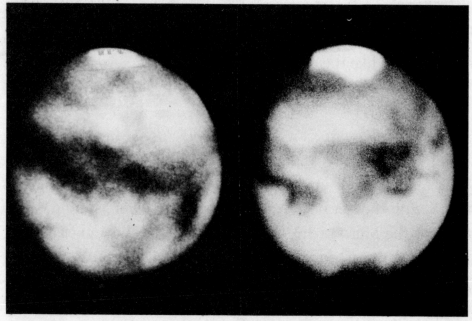

Opposite Hemispheres of Mars in 1956

As Mars travels around the sun more slowly than the earth, we catch up to it and pass it about every 26 months. That is 2 years and 2 months. The earth comes between Mars and the sun. Thus, Mars can be seen in the night sky, directly opposite to the position of the sun. At such times, the whole bright side of Mars faces the earth and we have our best opportunity to observe the planet.

When it comes close, Mars can be within 35 million miles of the earth. It can be as far away as 63 million miles. Then Mars appears as a bright red object in the sky all night long. It is highest above the horizon about midnight.

Astronomers have used every chance to study the surface of Mars. The red color of the planet is caused by light being reflected from the vast orange-colored areas which appear to be deserts or dust-covered plains. Other areas of Mars appear dark brown at times and dark green at other times. The changes in color in these darker areas come at the times when there are changes in the Martian seasons. Mars goes through seasons just like the earth's, except that Mars' seasons are twice as long as ours. Mars takes twice as long as the earth to go around the sun.

The changes in color that take place on Mars have made some people believe that there may be life on Mars. They think it is some form of low plant-life that grows, dies, and changes color with the seasons. Temperatures are lower than on earth. During the Martian day they are just a little above the freezing point of water. On the coldest nights the temperature is about 150 degrees below zero Fahrenheit. Near the equator, at noon, the temperature can get up to about 80 degrees Fahrenheit.

JUPITER AND SATURN

Jupiter is the largest of the planets, eleven times the size of the earth. Saturn is the second largest, 9 times the earth's size. It is also the planet with the strange rings around its equator.

These rings are 175,000 miles across, but probably less than 100 miles thick. Both planets are quite far from the sun and are very cold. They are always far from the earth, but they are so large that they appear very bright in our sky. Although Jupiter and Saturn are revolving around the sun, they move so slowly that it takes several weeks to notice a change in their positions among the stars.

Saturn and ring system

Both Jupiter and Saturn are strangely light for planets as large as they are. Both are probably made up mostly of frozen gases, with only small solid cores of rock or metal many thousand miles below the surface we observe. Bands of green and yellow, and occasional orange and red spots, are observed on both planets. They show us that these planets are spinning very fast.

URANUS, NEPTUNE AND PLUTO

Uranus and Neptune are both about four times larger than the earth but they are so far from the earth and so faint that they cannot be observed except with a large telescope. They are also largely made up of frozen gases like Jupiter and Saturn. The most distant planet, Pluto, is so far away that it can only be detected by careful examination of photographs of the heavens. Very little is known about it. It was not discovered until 1930. It appears to be about the size of the earth, or smaller, which is strange since it is far out in the solar system, in the realm of the giant planets.

Pluto takes about 248 years to go around the sun, and it has not moved very far from the position it had in the sky when it was discovered. It actually comes closer to the sun than Neptune at one point. The orbit of Pluto is tilted quite a bit to the orbits of the other planets so there is no danger that it may collide with Neptune.

THE ASTEROIDS

The asteroids are small members of the sun's family located in the space between Mars and Jupiter, the fourth and fifth planets out from the sun. The region where they revolve around the sun is sometimes called the Asteroid Belt. Almost two thousand asteroids have been discovered. The largest one, Ceres, is about 480 miles in diameter. There are probably several thousand smaller ones that have not been found. Some are less than a half mile across.

Asteroids are sometimes called "minor planets" by astronomers. When a new one is found, it may be reported as the discovery of a minor planet. Some people will misinterpret this and wonder if there are then ten planets in the solar system instead of the nine which are listed. If the asteroids were included among the list of planets, there would be many more than ten, probably closer to two thousand. Although asteroids are very much like planets—small, solid bodies revolving around the sun and shining only by reflected sunlight, they are put in a different class. We know of only nine major planets.

COMETS

The strangest of all the captives of the sun are the comets. When some comets approach close to the sun, they become quite brilliant and spectacular objects with long, beautiful tails. The tails caused people to name them "hairy stars" which is what the word comet meant long ago.

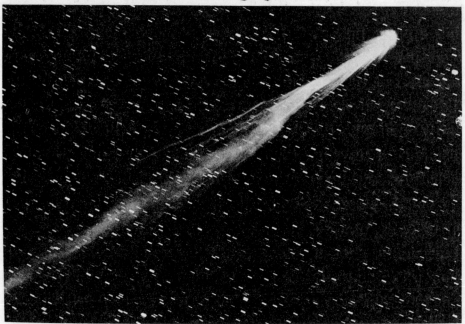

Moorehause's Comet 1908

Astronomers are still not sure just what comets are or where they come from. They appear to be collections of rocks or stones and chunks of ice moving around the sun in very long, almost cigar-shaped, orbits. They travel very rapidly when they come close to the sun. At the other end of their orbits, billions of miles away from the sun, comets travel very slowly. Far from the sun, comets are invisible. They grow bright only when they approach the sun.

As a comet approaches the sun, the energy of the sun is absorbed in the ice and stone collection which makes up the comet's head. This energy sets free gases which expand and cause the head of the comet to become bright and star-like. When this happens the comet may be discovered by some astronomer using a telescope. As it comes closer to the sun, the gases will be forced away from the comet by the pressure of sunlight, and a comet's tail will develop which anyone can see. Have you ever seen a comet?

The tail sweeps around the sun with the comet, always pointing away from the sun. It grows until the comet starts going away from the sun again. Then the tail slowly disappears and the comet again becomes a dim object far out in space. It may not return to the sun again for many years.

Very bright comets are rare, but sometimes, as in 1910 and 1957, several may be seen in a single year. One of the two bright comets in 1910 was the famous Halley's Comet, which returns close to the sun every 75 or 76 years. It will be back again in 1986. If it lives up to its fame, it should be well worth seeing. During its appearance in 1910, it extended over 15 million miles. Because it passed so close to the earth, it was a giant in the sky, bright enough to be seen even in the daytime.

METEORS — "SHOOTING STARS"

Comets are believed to be responsible for another kind of sky display, called a meteor. A meteor is a streak of light in the nighttime sky. It is the kind of thing which most people call a "falling star" or a "shooting star."

These objects are not really stars. They are tiny bits of solid material which were once flying around the sun in the space between the planets. There are countless billions of them. When we see them, the particles race through the air above the earth at speeds of about 25 miles per second. This is so fast that each particle heats up and becomes a gas. A streak of light results.

Willamette Meteorite and young girl

The name meteorite is given to pieces of solid material found on earth which were once meteors on their journey from outer space toward the earth. They are samples of the material flying through space. Thousands of meteorites have been found, most of them made up of solid iron, with a little nickel mixed with it. A few are made up of stony material.

The larger meteorites are displayed in museums or planetariums. The largest one in any museum is on display at the American Museum-Hayden Planetarium in New York. It weighs 34 tons and 85 pounds. You can read this weight yourself when you visit the Hayden Planetarium because this giant meteorite stands on a special scale.

On certain nights of the year, the earth seems to run into a large swarm of meteoroid particles. Then you can observe a meteor shower. This is the kind of thing which astronomers think is caused by a comet. As a comet sweeps around the sun, it distributes a lot of comet dust in space, filling its orbit with a stream of very fine particles.

Comets and meteoroids travel around the sun, but they violate the very neat arrangement found in most of the large members of the sun's family. The planets and their satellites all travel around the sun in the same level or plane, at nearly the same level where the earth's orbit is found. All the planets and most of their satellites also travel around the sun in the same direction. But the comets and meteoroids are found travelling around between the planets in almost any level and direction.

Prominent Meteor Showers Which Take Place Each Year

Name of Shower	Date when most meteors are observed	Meteors seem to radiate from this position
Quadrantids	Jan. 3	Northern sky between Hercules and North Star, in early morning hours.
Lyrids	Apr. 22	Near bright star Vega, in northeast in morning skies.
May Aquarids	May 5	Southeast in morning sky.
Delta Aquarids	July 29	Southeastern sky in early morning, not far from Fomalhaut.
Perseids	Aug. 12	Best shower, usually. Look in northeast after midnight.
Orionids	Oct. 20	Eastern sky after midnight, just north of Betelguese.
Leonids	Nov. 16	In the Lion's head, north of Regulus. Look in northeast in morning sky.
Geminids	Dec. 12	Near Castor and Pollux, high in northeast after midnight.

All these captives of the sun, from the largest planet to the smallest particle of space dust, obey the same laws. They all travel in elliptical paths with the sun at one focus. They all travel faster as they come closer to the sun. All will be studied better when man himself is no longer a captive of the earth, but free to explore the mysteries of space.

Star clouds in the Milky Way

The greatest adventure of all with the stars is to discover them for yourself. When you are able to call out the names of the bright stars and prominent constellations you will have a wonderful hobby. You will want to find and know a few more until almost every star you see is familiar. Why not begin tonight?

Some stars are in the sky every night. Those are the ones you should get to know first. They are in the north and appear to circle the north pole of the sky during the night. That is why they are known as the circumpolar stars.

FINDING CIRCUMPOLAR STARS

The easiest stars to find are the ones in the northern part of the sky, because they are always there. They are the stars that are nearly overhead at the earth's north pole. They include the bright North Star, the figure of the Big Dipper and the Little Dipper, and the five-starred group called Cassiopeia (kas-ee-oh-*pea*-ah). They are not always found in the same place, but they are always above the horizon for most of the United States.

First look for the Big Dipper. It has seven stars—three in the handle and four in the bowl. It is a large group, covering a wide area in the sky. Starting from the end of the bowl, the stars are named Alkaid (*al*-kade), Mizar (*my*-czar), Alioth (al-ee-*oth*), Megrez (*meg*-rez), Phecda (*fek*-dah), Merak (*mee*-rack), and Dubhe (*dubb*-ee). Early at night in April and May it is high in the sky toward the north. In the summer, on the nights of July and August, it is in the northwest, with the bowl down and the handle curving upward. In the early evenings of November and December, it is low in the north. By February and March, it appears in the northeast, with the handle pointing downward and the bowl uppermost.

No matter what time of year you see it, however, the Big Dipper always looks the same. That is why stars are often spoken of as "fixed" that is, not moving. The stars actually are moving rapidly through space, but they are so far away that the pictures and shapes in which they are arranged never seem to change. The earth too is moving on its journey around the sun. In July we are about 186 million miles away from where we were in December. But even that great distance does not change the arrangement of the stars enough to affect their appearance. The stars are "fixed" because a star pattern like the Big Dipper looked almost the same a thousand years ago as it does today. It will look the same a thousand years from now.

But in another sense the stars are not fixed. They are not always found in the same part of the sky. The reason for that is quite simple. We on earth are spinning around beneath them, so they appear to drift overhead in a direction opposite to our motion. As the earth spins us around toward east once a day, the stars drift toward the west, also going around the sky once each day. Some stars rise and some set, but those in the north, above the north pole, go around and around in circles.

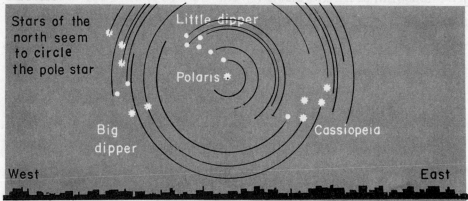

The point above our north pole is at the center of each star's circle. We call it the north pole of the sky. Once you have found the Big Dipper, you have an excellent guide to the other groups in the northern sky.

The North Star and the Little Dipper are easy to find. You can locate the North Star by using the Pointers. These are the two end stars, Merak and Dubhe, in the bowl of the Big Dipper. A line from Merak to Dubhe points to the North Star. It is the first bright star beyond Dubhe along the line. The North Star is known as Polaris (*pole*-a-riss). When you face toward Polaris, you are facing toward the north pole, which means that you are facing north. The North Star is also the end star in the handle of the Little Dipper.

The stars of the two dippers and the other circumpolar stars just seem to go around in circles all year long. But the positions of the stars in the rest of the sky change during the year. Since the earth is carrying us around the sun once a year, we are taken on a tour to look at different groups of stars as the seasons of the year change. During the year, the scene in the sky shifts slowly westward. This change should not be confused with the rising and setting of the stars every night. The seasonal shift is caused by the earth's revolution about the sun. The nightly changes are caused by the earth's rotation on its axis.

The stars that we see in the eastern half of the sky soon after sundown on the nights from March to June are known as the Spring Stars. Likewise those first appearing in the east early at night from June to September are the Stars of the Summer. In the same way, the Stars of the Autumn are those we see from September to December and the Stars of the Winter are those we see from December to March. The sky pictures on the following pages show you what stars you can find in the eastern half of the sky early on the nights of each season. The long arrows are your guide lines or pointers.

94

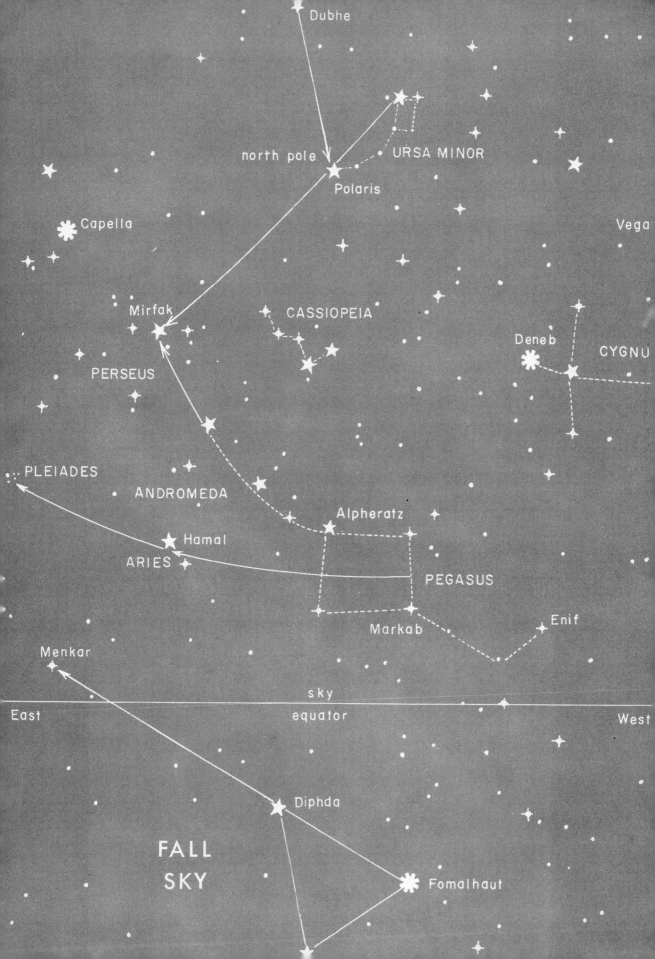

THE STARS OF THE MILKY WAY

Have you ever observed the Milky Way? Have you ever wondered what causes those patches of hazy light that form a pathway across the sky on almost every clear, dark night? The light of the Milky Way comes from millions of stars too far away to be seen by your unaided eye as separate stars.

A telescope will show you some of the stars that make up the Milky Way. It will show you that there are many more

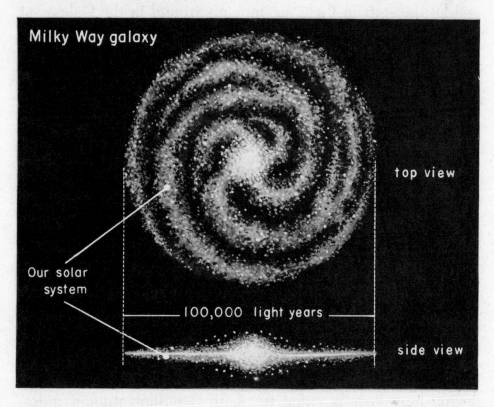

Milky Way galaxy

top view

Our solar system

100,000 light years

side view

stars along the Milky Way than in any other direction in the sky. This is the clue to the way in which all the stars we can see are organized. The Milky Way is the edge or rim of the enormous "City" of stars that makes up our Galaxy, sometimes called the Milky Way Galaxy.

99

Every star in this "City" of stars, the sun included, belongs to the Milky Way Galaxy. The stars of the Galaxy are arranged as shown in the illustration. The Galaxy is flat and rather thin, when viewed from the side, but round like a plate when seen from above or below. The stars are not distributed evenly throughout the Galaxy. There is a large cloud of stars in the center and most of the other stars are collected in smaller clouds that form arms winding around the center. These arms and all the stars in them are moving around in the Galaxy, at speeds of hundreds of miles per second. Our sun is located off to one side of the Galaxy. It is about ⅔ of the way from the center to the edge and on the inner rim of one of the arms.

Have you any idea how large The Galaxy is and how far away the stars really are? Distances in the space between the stars are so great that astronomers do not use miles to measure them. They invented a new measure of distance called a light year. A light year sounds like a unit of time, but it isn't. It is the distance that light would travel in one year. Light waves travel at a speed of 186,000 miles per second. It takes the light of the sun about 8 light minutes to reach the earth. The sun is 8 light minutes away. As you know, that is about 93 million miles. The light from the next nearest star takes about 4½ years to reach the earth, so that star is 4½ light years away. That's about 26 million million miles.

One light year is equal to about 6 million million miles, because that is how far light waves travel in one year. Can you imagine how far that is? A trip around the world at the equator would be a journey of 25,000 miles. That sounds like a long trip, but light would travel that far in less than 1/8th of a second. A light year is equal to about 240 million trips around the earth's equator.

Now take another look at the picture of The Galaxy. The distance across, from edge-to-edge, is about 100,000 light years. The distance through, from top to bottom is about 10,000 light years. The sun is about 35,000 light years from the center. The star nearest to the sun is Alpha Centauri. We cannot see it from the United States because it is too far down in the southern hemisphere of the sky. The nearest star that you can see without a telescope is Sirius, the brightest star in the sky. Sirius is about 8 light years away from the earth.

You would expect that the brightest stars would also be the nearest stars. That is generally but not completely true. There are about 6,000 stars near enough and bright enough so that you can see them without a telescope. On a clear, dark night, you can see about 3,000 of them. But all of these stars are not close. And there are some close stars which we cannot see at all. The reason is that all stars do not have the same brightness. Some stars look bright because they are close, others at greater distances happen to be so bright that we can see them just as easily.

The sun is a star of about average brightness. It is just about average in all respects. It is a yellowish star, with a surface temperature of 10,000 degrees Fahrenheit. Its diameter is 864,000 miles. Some stars have temperatures much higher, some lower; some stars are thousands of times as large, and others are only a small fraction of the sun's size; and the colors of the stars range all the way from red to yellow and blue.

The color of a star shows how hot it is. The hotter a star is, the bluer will be its light. Low temperature stars are faint red. Betelguese, Aldebaran, and Antares are red stars. Therefore, they are cool stars. Average stars, like the sun and Sirius, are yellow. Capella, Pollux, and Polaris are other yellow stars. And hot stars, with surface temperatures of 50,000 degrees or more, are blue-white. Vega, Rigel, and Spica are bluish stars. Look at some of the brighter stars and see if you can identify their colors. The colors of the stars are much easier to observe with a telescope or a pair of binoculars.

SEEING STARS WITH A TELESCOPE

Some stars are not really just one star, but maybe two or more. For example, Sirius is a star with a companion. Polaris, Aldebaran, Rigel, Regulus, and Antares, are double stars. Castor actually has six stars circling around one another where your eyes see only one. Many double stars can be seen in a small telescope. Finding and identifying them can be a lot of fun. The two stars are usually of different colors, so that the observer has two things, color and brightness, to watch for when he searches for double stars.

Another very interesting field of work for amateurs with a small telescope is a study of variable stars. These are stars which change their brightness.

Some variable stars change their brightness because they are double stars, one brighter than the other. If the two stars pass one another as we look at them, then the brighter star will grow fainter while the darker star partly covers it. Algol, a very well known star, changes its brightness this way. It is in the constellation Perseus. About once every 3 days it becomes less than half as bright as normal.

Most of the variable stars seem to change in brightness because of some quality of the star itself. Polaris and Betelguese are examples. Some of these stars change in brightness very rapidly, in only a few hours. Others have a period of change that requires several days. Still others require very long periods to go through their changes. An excellent example

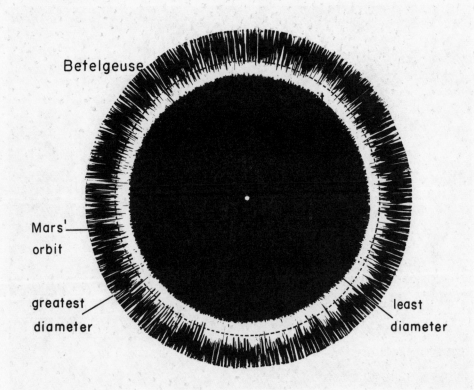

Betelgeuse, a red giant star, changes size as it changes brightness

is the star called Mira, which means wonderful. Mira was the first star discovered to be variable. It takes almost a year to go through its changes. If you would like to find Mira, the most famous of the variable stars, you should look at the sky in autumn. It is in the constellation Cetus. The V-shaped nose of Taurus points almost directly toward it. But do not be surprised if you can't see it. Mira fades to invisibility for months at a time.

103

There is one special kind of variable star which surprises everyone when it changes its brightness. This kind suddenly flares up many thousands of times brighter than usual. Then it fades out again in a few weeks or a few months. Such stars were called *novae* which means new stars because that is what

Taurus. Crab Nebula

they were thought to be. We now realize that they are not new at all but stars that had always been there, faint and far away. They became novae when suddenly they exploded and grew much brighter than usual. When one of these exploding stars increases many millions of times in brightness it is called a *supernova*. A supernova can become as bright as Venus, so bright that it can be seen even in the daytime. The last supernova observed was several hundred years ago.

104

BEYOND THE MILKY WAY

All the stars you see in the sky, the Milky Way, and many more stars you cannot see, belong to The Galaxy in which we live. What lies beyond? Beyond in the nearly empty, starless space that surrounds our galaxy are other galaxies. There are millions of them, each with its own billions of stars. With a small telescope, we cannot see the individual stars in these other galaxies beyond the Milky Way. We see the entire galaxies as faint clouds of light. But with a large telescope, with a camera attached, we can take pictures that show us how they are shaped and how the stars within them are arranged.

Spiral Galaxies in Leo

Some of these exterior galaxies are arranged like a pinwheel. These are called spiral galaxies. We believe our Galaxy is shaped like these other spiral galaxies.

105

Some distant galaxies are round and some are irregular in shape. Still others look like a long bar, with two trailing arms. Some are small, with only a few hundred million stars; others are large, like the Milky Way, with hundreds of billions of stars.

The nearest of the large galaxies and the only one visible in the Northern Hemisphere without a telescope can be seen in the autumn skies. You may have seen it, without realizing what it is. It looks like a very faint patch of light in the constellation Andromeda, just above the star Mirach. It is far beyond those stars in Andromeda through which we can see it. This Great Galaxy in Andromeda is believed to be over 2 million light years away. If you have ever wondered what is the farthest thing you can see with your eyes, this is it!

Great Nebula in Andromeda

All of the hundreds of millions of galaxies in the universe seem to be moving away from one another at very high speeds. No one has explained why. No one really knows where they are expanding to, or where they came from. All of the hundreds of millions of distant galaxies are observed to be moving away from us and from one another at speeds which increase with their distances. This means that the universe is expanding.

Maybe someday astronomy will be able to tell us why the universe is expanding and what, if anything, lies beyond these galaxies. Astronomy is a science. It has given us answers to many mysteries, but some are still unsolved. Have you thought of a career in astronomy? Perhaps you are one of those who some day will advance still further what man knows about space and the stars.

Spiral Nebula in Canes Venatici

9 Things You Might Want to Know

More people are interested in astronomy than in any other science. It is taught in colleges, high schools, and even in grade schools in our country. There are probably more amateur astronomers than there are amateurs in any other field of physical science.

If you think you might like to be an astronomer, you should know something about the kind of work they do, how to prepare yourself, and the kind of opportunities astronomy offers.

Many astronomers do research — learning the basic facts about stars, planets, space. Research is the goal of all astronomers, because research leads to new knowledge about the universe. The astronomers who do research work at observatories must use telescopes, telescope accessories, and complicated measuring instruments in their work.

Other astronomers spend most of their time in teaching at colleges or universities. They may do some research during summers.

The third kind of work astronomers do is in technology. Many government and industrial projects of today, especially projects using rockets and missiles, require the help of astronomers.

A great many astronomers, over 60%, developed their interest in the subject *before* they went to college. So, if you want to be an astronomer, develop your interest now. You will have to go to college, and only students who have done well in school get in. Take as much mathematics and science as you can. But don't neglect English (astronomers have to explain their work) and study a foreign language.

You can improve your chances of becoming an astronomer by reading, studying, observing, and learning astronomy. Make it your hobby and keep up your interest in it.

If you are serious about becoming an astronomer, you will have to obtain a doctor's degree. This will mean at least three years of study and research after graduation from college.

After receiving his doctor's degree, the young astronomer will find many types of work open to him. The demand for the special skill and training of astronomers is growing. Which kind of astronomical work would you prefer? Now is the time to start preparing for it.

BOOKS YOU MAY WANT TO READ

ALL ABOUT ROCKETS AND JETS. Fletcher Pratt. Random House.

ALL ABOUT THE STARS. Anne Terry White. Random House.

THE BIG BOOK OF SPACE. Earl Oliver Hurst. Grosset & Dunlap.

THE BOY'S BOOK OF SPACE. Patrick Moore. Roy Publishers.

COMETS. Herbert S. Zim. William Morrow & Co.

THE EARTH SATELLITE. John Lewellen. Alfred A. Knopf.

EXPERIMENTS IN THE PRINCIPLES OF SPACE TRAVEL.
   Franklyn M. Branley. Thomas Y. Crowell Co.

EXPLORING BY SATELLITE. Franklyn M. Branley. Thomas Y. Crowell Co.

EXPLORING MARS. Roy A. Gallant. Garden City Books.

EXPLORING THE MOON. Roy A. Gallant. Garden City Books.

EXPLORING THE UNIVERSE. Roy A. Gallant. Garden City Books.

FIND THE CONSTELLATIONS. H. A. Rey. Houghton Mifflin Co.

THE FIRST BOOK OF SPACE TRAVEL. Jeanne Bendick. Franklin Watts.

FUN WITH ASTRONOMY. Mae and Ira Freeman. Random House.

GALILEO, FIRST OBSERVER OF MARVELOUS THINGS.
   Elma Ehrlich Levinger. Julian Messner, Inc.

THE GOLDEN BOOK OF ASTRONOMY. Rose Wyler and Gerald Ames.
   Simon & Schuster.

MARS. Franklyn M. Branley. Thomas Y. Crowell Co.

OBSERVING THE HEAVENS. Peter Hood. Oxford University Press.

OUR STARLAND. C. C. Wylie. Lyons & Carnahan.

PATTERNS IN THE SKY. W. Maxwell Reed. William Morrow & Co.

PICTURE BOOK OF ASTRONOMY. Jerome S. Meyer. Lothrop, Lee & Shepard.

PLANETS, STARS AND SPACE. Joseph Miles Chamberlain and Thomas D. Nicholson. Creative Educational Society.

THE REAL BOOK ABOUT SPACE TRAVEL. Hal Goodwin. Garden City Books.

THE REAL BOOK ABOUT STARS. Hal Goodwin. Garden City Books.

ROCKETS, JETS, GUIDED MISSILES AND SPACE SHIPS. Jack Coggins and Fletcher Pratt. Randon House.

ROCKETS, MISSILES, AND MOONS. Charles Coombs. William Morrow & Co.

SECRETS OF SPACE FLIGHT. Lloyd Mallan. Arco Pub.

SOLAR ENERGY. Franklyn M. Branley. Thomas Y. Crowell Co.

SPACE SATELLITE, The Story of the Man-Made Moon. Lee Beeland and Robert Wells. Prentice-Hall, Inc.

THE SPANGLED HEAVENS. Lawrence Edwards. Distributed by The Macmillan Co.

SPEEDING INTO SPACE. Marie Neurath. Lothrop, Lee & Shepard.

STAR STORIES. Gertrude Chandler Warner. Pilgrim Press.

STAR OF WONDER. Robert R. Coles and Frances Frost. McGraw-Hill.

STARS. Herbert S. Zim and Robert H. Baker. Simon & Schuster.

THE STARS: STEPPING STONES INTO SPACE. Irving Adler. The John Day Co.

THE STORY OF OUR CALENDAR. Ruth Brindze. Vanguard Press.

SUN, MOON AND PLANETS. Roy K. Marshall. Henry Holt & Co.

SUN, MOON AND STARS. William T. Skilling and Robert S. Richardson. McGraw-Hill.

THIS WAY TO THE STARS. John Schealer. E. P. Dutton & Co.

THE TRUE BOOK OF MOON, SUN AND STARS. John Lewellen. Childrens Press.

WONDERS AROUND THE SUN. Mary Graham Bonner. Lantern Press, Inc.

WONDERS OF SPACE STAMPS. Hubert Bernhard. Simon & Schuster.

WORLDS AROUND US. Patrick Moore. Abelard-Schuman.

THE WORLD IN SPACE. Alexander Marshack. Thomas Nelson & Sons.

WORLDS IN THE SKY. Carroll Lane Fenton and Mildren Adams Fenton. John Day Co.

YOU AMONG THE STARS. Herman and Nina Schneider. William R. Scott, Inc.

YOU AND SPACE TRAVEL. John Lewellen. Childrens Press.

INDEX

Satchel PAIGE

Striking Out Jim Crow

by James Sturm
& Rich Tommaso

with an introduction by Gerald Early

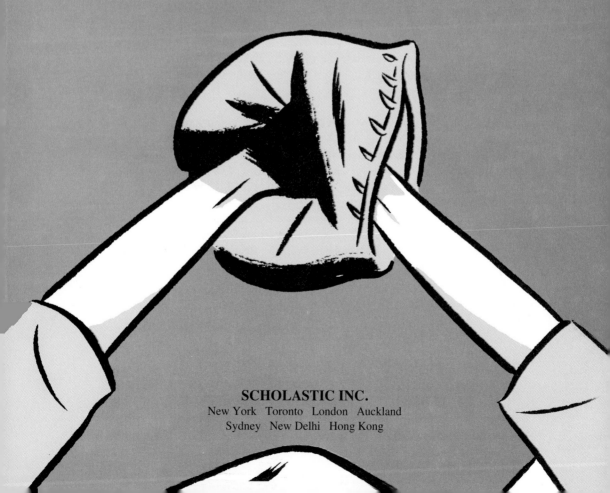

SCHOLASTIC INC.
New York Toronto London Auckland
Sydney New Delhi Hong Kong

Publication design by James Sturm and Michel Vrána.
Production Assistants: Joe Lambert, Amandine Maillarbaux, and Peter Wallis.

ISBN-13: 978-0-545-34474-6
ISBN-10: 0-545-34474-3

6 7 8 9 10   40   20 19 18 17 16 15 14

Introduction

by Gerald Early

He stood six foot three and one-half inches. Lanky, with big hands and big feet. He would walk across the field to the pitcher's mound in the middle of a game knowing everyone had come to see him, was waiting for him. He would sometimes do "shadow" tricks with the ball while warming up, joke around, act as if he wasn't very serious about playing the game. But he was serious indeed when he began his windup to throw the first pitch.

When he played, he took no prisoners. He was the master of his pitches and the master of the head game of keeping batters off balance. For underneath his playfulness was a fierce, proud competitor. He was the prince of pitchers, the smiling, smirking god of black baseball. He was the most popular black baseball player in the country from the 1920s to the 1940s. He was the most photographed of all Negro League players and the highest paid. His name was Leroy Paige.

His nickname was "Satchel" because as a child he had worked hustling luggage at a train station. Satchel was a fitting name, for he spent most of his adult life traveling around the United States and the Caribbean, playing baseball. "Have glove, will travel" could have been his motto. "I'll pitch until I die" could have been another one, as he pitched professionally until he was in his mid-sixties.

Once upon a time in the United States, African Americans could not play on baseball teams with whites. The two races were segregated by law and by custom for nearly seventy years. During this time, African Americans had to endure insult, inferior treatment, and harsh conditions, even violence, from whites. But in the legendary days of the national pastime, blacks loved baseball as much as whites did, and since they could not play with whites, they formed their own teams. They even formed their own professional leagues.

Black baseball developed a thrilling style and became its own world. It was a fast-paced game of stolen bases, bunts, line drives, and clever base-running. The players made more money than the average black person at that time, often a lot more. But black baseball was no easy game to play; not only was it competitive, but the conditions were tough. Black ballplayers barnstormed relentlessly, going anywhere to play any professional or semiprofessional team. This made it tough for the leagues to succeed, because the teams could make more money playing nonleague games. Sometimes black teams would play three games in a day.

Umpiring was often not the best. The condition of the fields left much to be desired. Crowds were frequently rowdy, and travel was hard because of segregation. Blacks could not use public restrooms, eat at most restaurants, or stay at virtually any

hotel not in a black neighborhood. They had to ride from city to city on broken-down buses, not on trains, as white major league teams did. But these men loved the game and played it with great passion and skill. It was in this world and among these men that Satchel Paige lived his life.

Satchel Paige was born on July 7, 1905(?) in Mobile, Alabama. No one is sure of this date because Paige never told the truth about his age, and at the time the South did not keep very accurate birth records for African Americans. He was born into a poor family of twelve. Always pitching rocks at squirrels and rabbits to get extra meat for the family dinner table, Paige started pitching baseballs in school when he was ten. He began to pitch as a professional in 1924 and made it his life's work. He was sensational as a young pitcher, with a blazing fastball and wicked curve, so remarkable that as the years went by he became famous beyond just Negro League fans. He became so famous that people came just to see him pitch. Paige, realizing he was a star attraction, soon began to jump around from team to team

He was sensational as a young pitcher, with a blazing fastball and wicked curve, so remarkable that as the years went by he became famous beyond just Negro League fans. He became so famous that people came just to see him pitch.

to increase his salary. Sometimes he would pitch for several teams in the same year.

The Negro Leagues found it hard to stop their star players from doing that, and Paige did it more than anyone. The two teams that Paige became most associated with were the Pittsburgh Crawfords and the Kansas City Monarchs.

Jackie Robinson became the first black to play for the major leagues when he started for the Brooklyn Dodgers in 1947. In 1948, Satchel signed with the Cleveland Indians. He was forty-two, an age at which most players would have already retired.

The graphic novel you hold in your hands tells a bit of the story of Satchel Paige and the men of the Negro Leagues. It tells the story of what this game meant to the men who played it and to the people who watched it. For many of the black men who played, baseball was the great American Dream made real. Satchel Paige was one of those men, a great athlete and pioneer, who helped to make the ballparks of America level playing fields for everyone.

—G.E.

Satchel
PAIGE

1929 AIN'T EASY LEAVIN' YOUR WIFE AND CHILD, BUT YOU CAN'T BE A BALLPLAYER UNLESS YOU WILLIN' TO TRAVEL.

FRANCES DON'T LIKE MY LEAVIN', BUT SHE'S AGREE-ABLE TO IT. SHE KNOWS WHEN I GET BACK, MY POCKETS WILL BE FULL. SHE CAN SPEND ALL HER TIME RAISIN' OUR BABY AND NOT SOME WHITE MAN'S KIDS.

I'M 18 YEARS OLD, AND I'LL BE MAKIN' MORE MONEY THAN HER DADDY AND MY DADDY PUT TOGETHER. AIN'T BRAGGIN' IF IT'S TRUE.

INSTEAD OF BRINGIN' HOME FORTY CENTS A DAY WORKIN' MR. JENNINGS'S FIELDS, I'LL BE MAKIN' SEVENTEEN DOLLARS A WEEK. MR. JENNINGS SURE MAKES THAT KIND OF MONEY BUT NO NEGRO THAT I KNOW.

TUCKWILLA, ALABAMA, IS COTTON COUNTRY. SHARE-CROPPER SHACKS EVERY WHICH WAY YOU LOOK.

NO SPECIAL CARE AS TO HOW THEY WAS BUILT 'CAUSE THEY WAS BUILT FOR NEGROES.

MAKE ME SOME MONEY, AND I'LL BUILD ME A REAL HOUSE FOR MY FAMILY. THEM SHACKS IS GETTIN' TOO SMALL FOR ME.

I ARRIVE IN MEMPHIS FIRST THING IN THE MORNIN' AND PLAY A DOUBLEHEADER THAT DAY AGAINST THE ST. LOUIS STARS. OVER THE NEXT TWO WEEKS, WE PLAY GAMES IN MONTGOMERY, TUSCALOOSA, AND SELMA. THE RED SOX LOSE PLENTY MORE THAN THEY WIN, BUT NOT ON ACCOUNT OF ME. I MAY BE THE YOUNGEST PLAYER ON THE TEAM, BUT NOBODY HITS THE BALL ANY BETTER.

TODAY WE TRAVELIN' TO PLAY THE BIRMINGHAM BLACK BARONS. SATCHEL PAIGE WILL BE PITCHIN'.

PAIGE AIN'T BUT A FEW YEARS OLDER THAN ME AND HE GETTIN' HIS NAME READ IN THE **CHICAGO DEFENDER** AND THE **PITTSBURGH COURIER.** YOU GET IN THE PAPERS, AND YOU MAKE A NAME FOR YOURSELF.

PEOPLE SAY HE'S THE NEXT BULLET ROGAN. LOOKS LIKE ROGAN, HARD THROWER LIKE ROGAN.

BIG CROWD AT RICKWOOD FIELD. BIGGEST CROWD I EVER PLAYED BEFORE. HOPE THERE ARE SOME NEWSPAPERMEN IN ATTENDANCE. I AIM TO SHOW EVERYONE I'M THE BEST, AND THE ONLY WAY TO GO ABOUT THAT IS TO BEAT THE BEST. MORE PEOPLE THAT SEE THAT, THE BETTER.

PAIGE'S CATCHER, BILL PERKINS, IS BUCKLIN' UP, BUT NO SIGN OF PAIGE.

NEARIN' GAME TIME AND THE PITCHER'S MOUND STILL EMPTY.

UMPIRE HEADS OVER TO THE BARONS' DUGOUT AND HAS A WORD WITH THE MANAGER.

UMPIRE YELLS, "PLAY BALL," AND LIKE EVERYONE ELSE IN THE PARK, I'M LOOKIN' FOR PAIGE.

THEN I SEE HIM, TALL AND LANKY, SHUFFLIN' ACROSS THE INFIELD. HARD TO BELIEVE THAT A MAN WHO MOVES SO SLOW CAN PITCH SO FAST.

PAIGE TAKES A FEW MINUTES ADJUSTIN' THE LACES IN HIS RIGHT SHOE.

NEXT, HIS SHIRT GETS TUCKED IN AND BELT BUCKLE TIGHTENED.

OUR LEADOFF HITTER, CONNIE WESLEY, STEPS INTO THE BATTER'S BOX. PERKINS STILL AIN'T TAKIN' HIS CROUCH.

NOW THE LEFT SHOELACE.

THEN A FEW MINUTES WORKIN' THE DIRT ON THE MOUND.

FINALLY, PAIGE IS READY TO PITCH. IF HE TOOK ANY WARM-UP TOSSES, I DIDN'T SEE IT.

HARD TO TELL IF PAIGE IS AWARE THAT THERE IS ANYONE ELSE IN THE STADIUM BESIDES HIMSELF.

SLOWLY, THEM BONY ARMS ARE RAISED TOWARD HEAVEN.

THEN SINK TO HIS CHEST.

THE BALL IN THE CATCHER'S MITT. PERKINS NOT MOVIN' HIS GLOVE AN INCH.

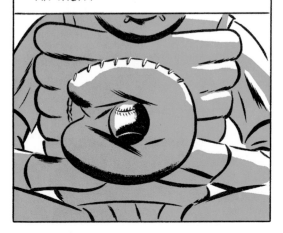

WESLEY NOT MOVIN' HIS BAT AN INCH EITHER. STRIKE ONE.

STRIKE TWO IS THE SAME PITCH, A LITTLE HIGHER IN THE STRIKE ZONE. WESLEY TAKES A CUT, MISSES BADLY.

FROM WHAT I CAN TELL, PERKINS AIN'T CALLIN' ANY PITCHES, HE JUST HOLDS OUT HIS MITT, AND PAIGE HITS IT WITH A FASTBALL.

WESLEY TRIES MOVIN' BACK IN THE BATTER'S BOX, CHOKES UP AN EXTRA INCH ON HIS BAT.

STRIKE THREE.

PAIGE WALKS AROUND THE MOUND AS INFIELDERS WHIRL THE BALL AROUND HIM.

I STEP UP TO THE PLATE.

PAIGE PAYS ME LITTLE MIND. ALL HIS ATTENTION NOW ON HIS SHOELACES.

WELL, TWO CAN PLAY AT THAT GAME. WHEN HE'S FINALLY READY TO PITCH, I CALL FOR TIME AND STEP OUT OF THE BOX.

AFTER MAKIN' PAIGE WAIT ON ME FOR A SPELL, I MOVE BACK INTO THE BOX.

I LOOK UP TO SEE PAIGE LOOKIN' AT ME, SHAKIN' HIS HEAD LIKE HE MY DADDY WAITIN' ON HIS FUSSY CHILD TO SETTLE DOWN. WHO IS HE TO SHOW ME UP LIKE THAT?

I KEEP MY HANDS LOOSE AND MY EYES LOCKED ON PAIGE'S THROWIN' HAND AS HE BEGINS HIS WINDUP.

LOTS OF MOVIN' PARTS: LEGS FLYIN' ONE WAY, ARMS ANOTHER, DISAPPEARIN' BEHIND THAT LEG, EVERYTHIN' CHUGGIN' AT A DIFFERENT SPEED.

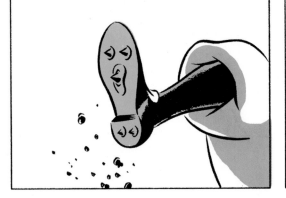

THEN THE ARM COMES OUT AROUND, AND YOU CATCH A GLIMPSE OF THAT BALL...

LOOKS LIKE AN ASPIRIN TABLET STREAKIN' ACROSS THE PLATE, LOOKS LIKE A BASEBALL IN THE CATCHER'S MITT.

PAIGE'S MOUTH NOW MOVIN' AS QUICK AS HIS PITCHES.

LET HIM WORK HIS JAW -- I AIN'T GONNA GIVE HIM THE SATISFACTION. I TURN ASIDE.

GRIPPIN' THE BAT, I TELL MY HANDS TO RELAX. IF MY GRIP IS TOO TIGHT, MEANS I'M WOUND UP.

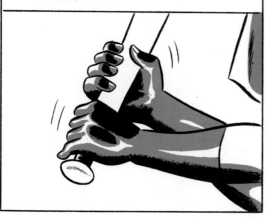

AIN'T A PERSON IN THIS STADIUM WHO DON'T KNOW WHAT PITCH IS COMIN'.

I START ROLLIN' THE WRISTS TO GET THE BAT MOVIN', THEN START MY SWING BEFORE I SEE THAT BALL.

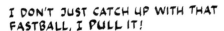
I DON'T JUST CATCH UP WITH THAT FASTBALL, I PULL IT!

I'M HALFWAY DOWN THE FIRST-BASE LINE BEFORE I HEAR THE UMPIRE YELL, "FOUL BALL!"

PAIGE HEADS ME OFF BEFORE I GET BACK TO THE PLATE, TRYIN' TO SHAKE MY HAND, CONGRATULATIN' ME. CONGRATULATIN' ME ON A FOUL BALL!

HE PLAYIN' TO THE CROWD, SHOWIN' ME UP! WHO IS HE TO SHOW ME UP LIKE THAT!?

I PICK UP MY BAT. PERKINS SMILES AND SAYS, "THAT'S SATCHEL'S BEE BALL, NOW YOU GONNA GET HIS JUMP BALL."

I'M WOUND UP NOW AND FIXED TO SPRING. NO FASTBALL GETTIN' BY ME.

PAIGE NOW STARTS WORRYIN' OVER HIS SHOELACES!

PAIGE TAKIN' HIS TIME, MAKIN' MY BLOOD HOTTER AND HOTTER.

I'M SQUEEZIN' THE BAT LIKE I'M CHOKIN' A CHICKEN. I TRY TO CALL TIME OUT, BUT PAIGE IS ALREADY INTO HIS WINDUP.

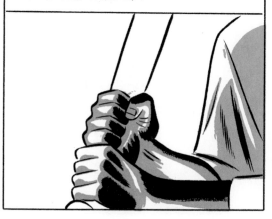

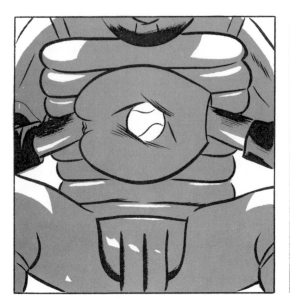

PAIGE WORKED ME UP TIGHT, ALL RIGHT. BALL IN THE CATCHER'S MITT BEFORE I COULD MOVE A MUSCLE.

LUCKY FOR ME, THE UMPIRE CALLS THE PITCH HIGH. ONE BALL, TWO STRIKES.

PAIGE NOW STARTS CLOWNIN' WITH HIS SECOND BASEMAN.

PAIGE MIGHT BEST ME TODAY, BUT I AIN'T GONNA BEAT MYSELF. HARD ENOUGH HITTIN' A BASEBALL WHEN YOU AIN'T ALL DISTRACTED.

GOT TO GET OUT OF PAIGE'S WAY OF DOIN' THINGS AND BACK TO MY OWN. I CALL FOR TIME AND STEP OUT OF THE BATTER'S BOX.

TAP MY RIGHT CLEAT THREE TIMES.
FIRST TAP HARD, THEN SOFTER AND
SOFTER.

SAME GOES FOR MY LEFT CLEAT.

PULL MY CAP AS LOW AS IT WILL
GO, LIKE PUTTIN' BLINDERS ON
A HORSE.

KEEP THE GRIP LOOSE, ROLL WRISTS,
LETTIN' THE BAT HEAD KEEP A NICE
EASY RHYTHM.

NO MORE THINKIN'.

BALL RICOCHETS OFF THE SHORTSTOP'S MITT INTO SHALLOW RIGHT FIELD. SECOND BASEMAN AND RIGHT FIELDER GO AFTER IT.

I'M HARD AROUND FIRST, LOOKIN' TO GRAB SECOND.

RIGHT FIELDER BARE-HANDS IT

AND COMES UP THROWIN'.

I'M IN UNDER THE TAG. EMMET WILSON GOT HIMSELF A DOUBLE! LET THEM NEWSPAPERMEN PUT THAT IN THEIR PAPERS!

SECOND BASE MAY AS WELL BE A MOUNTAINTOP, AND I EARNED MY RIGHT TO DO SOME SHOUTIN'! I TELL PAIGE WHAT I THINK OF HIS FASTBALL! BRING ON BULLET ROGAN! I'LL TAKE 'EM ALL ON!

NOW IT'S SATCHEL THAT'S TURNIN' AWAY. I KNOCKED THEM TAIL FEATHERS RIGHT OFF THAT PEACOCK!

GEORGE McALLISTER, OUR FIRST BASEMAN, STEPS UP TO THE PLATE.

I LOOK INTO OUR DUGOUT AND SEE THE COACH GIVIN' HIS SIGNS. KNOW WITHOUT LOOKIN' WHAT IT'S GOIN' TO BE. THE BOOK ON PAIGE: BUNT AND RUN, BUNT AND RUN.

I GET ME A HEALTHY LEAD OFF SECOND.

SOON AS HE STARTS RAISIN' THEM ARMS UP, I'M OFF. I AIN'T DONE DOIN' MY DAMAGE!

PAIGE'S MOTION MIGHT BE BEDEVILIN' TO HITTERS, BUT IT'S TO THE ADVANTAGE OF BASE RUNNERS!

MAC LAYS ONE DOWN, TRYIN' TO PUSH IT BETWEEN PAIGE AND FIRST.

PAIGE IS SURPRISINGLY FAST OFF THE MOUND.

FIRES TO FIRST FOR AN OUT.

I'M AROUND THIRD, GOT NO GET-BACK IN ME NOW. HOME PLATE IS CALLIN' ME LIKE A SWOLLEN HOLLER.

FIRST BASEMAN FIRES IT HOME.

PERKINS BLOCKIN' THE PLATE, BUT I'M COMIN' WITH EVERYTHIN' I GOT.

PERKINS, THICK AND HEAVY AS A PLOW MULE, HOLDIN' THAT BALL TIGHT.

BEFORE THE UMP CAN MAKE THE CALL, I SEE THE BALL ROLLIN' IN THE DUST. I SCORED A RUN ON SATCHEL PAIGE!

I TRY TO RISE AND CELEBRATE.

I HEAR THE UMP. "DON'T YOU MOVE, SON, WE GONNA GET SOME HELP."

A SHARP PAIN FILLS ME THROUGH AND THROUGH.

THINGS START FADIN' IN AND OUT, IN AND OUT. I OPEN MY EYES AND I SEE PAIGE OVER ME, SMILIN'.

HE'S HANDIN' ME THE BASEBALL.

"HERE YOU GO, BOY, A SOUVENIR OF YOUR PLAYIN' DAYS."

1934 Dizzy Dean wins thirty games for the St. Louis Cardinals.

Paige, with his crowd-pleasing fastball, is constantly on the road, pitching for the highest bidder.

Dean finishes his amazing season by defeating the Detroit Tigers in the seventh game of the World Series.

Dean then begins a two-month barnstorming tour, pitting his all-white team against Satchel Paige's Negro All-Stars.

Touring together, they pack major league stadiums. Dean makes more money with Paige than he does all season with the Cardinals.

As they pitch against one another, Paige, more often than not, gets the better of Dean.

1935 JENNINGS FIELD, TUCKWILLA, ALABAMA
MR. WALKER JENNINGS IS GIVIN' HIS TWIN SONS, WALLACE AND
WILLIAM, A BIG SEND-OFF, AND WHEN MR. JENNINGS THROWS A CELEBRATION
YOU BE SMART TO ATTEND.

COLOREDS ARE NOT ALLOWED DOWN NEAR THE INFIELD AND GRANDSTAND. WE SIT OUT BY THE OUTFIELD GRASS IN THE SHADE OF CARPENTER WOODS. CLOSEST I CAME TO A BASEBALL FIELD SINCE MY KNEE QUIT ON ME.

MY MOMMA WORKED IN THE JENNINGS'S HOME. WASHED THEM BOYS' CLOTHING, COOKED THEM THEIR FOOD. SAW MORE OF THEM LITTLE BOYS THAN SHE DID ME.

FROM WHERE WE AT YOU COULDN'T HEAR MR. JENNINGS'S SPEECH, BUT THE WHOLE TOWN KNOWS WHAT IT IS ABOUT. THE JENNINGS BOYS ARE TAKIN' THE EVENING TRAIN TO MISSOURI. THEY HAVE A TRYOUT WITH THE WORLD CHAMPION ST. LOUIS CARDINALS.

THEM TWINS GOOD. I WAS BETTER.

WHEN MR. JENNINGS FINISHES HIS SPEECH, EVERYBODY WHOOPS AND HOLLERS. THE BAND CLIMBS ONTO THE GAZEBO AND STRIKES UP "MEET ME IN ST. LOUIS."

MR. WALLACE WALKS ONTO THE FIELD AND PICKS UP THE BAT THAT WAS SITTING ON HOME PLATE.

MR. WILLIAM JOGS OUT PAST THE PITCHER'S MOUND, PAST SECOND BASE, AND INTO CENTER FIELD WHERE A BUCKET OF BASEBALLS WAITS FOR HIM.

MR. WILLIAM GOES INTO HIS WINDUP. HE'S GOIN' TO PITCH FROM OUT THERE, MORE THAN 200 FEET FROM THE PLATE.

NO CATCHER SETS UP BEHIND HOME PLATE.

EVERY PITCH COMES RIGHT DOWN MAIN STREET.

MR. WALLACE HITS EVERY PITCH, SPRAYIN' THE BALL ALL OVER THE FIELD. EACH BALL IS HIT FARTHER THAN THE ONE BEFORE.

THE LAST PITCH IS HIT THE HARDEST.

UP OVER THE OUTFIELD AND INTO CARPENTER WOODS--THAT BALL MUST HAVE TRAVELED OVER 450 FEET.

MY SON EMMET, JR. AND ANOTHER HALF DOZEN CHILDREN RACE INTO THEM WOODS LOOKIN' FOR THAT BALL.

ONE OF THE BOYS COME OUTTA THE WOODS WITH THAT BASEBALL. THEY ALL COULDN'T HAVE BEEN MORE EXCITED IF THEY'D DISCOVERED BURIED TREASURE.

ONLY BASEBALL A COLORED BOY KNOWS IS A WASHRAG TIED AROUND A ROCK. EVEN SOME OF THE ADULTS GATHER ROUND TO TAKE A LOOK.

ALL OF A SUDDEN, A LOUD WHISTLE.

IT'S MR. JENNINGS HIMSELF MAKIN' HIS WAY TOWARD US.

HE HOLDS OUT HIS HAND...

AND COLLECTS HIS BALL.

1941 Satchel Paige is the greatest box office attraction in baseball. Receiving a percentage of ticket sales, he is also the world's highest-paid athlete. Paige now takes to flying from game to game aboard a private DC-3 airplane.

National press coverage in LIFE and TIME introduces Paige to an even greater audience. White major league hitters, including Rogers Hornsby, Hack Wilson, Ted Williams, and Joe DiMaggio regard Paige as the toughest pitcher they ever faced.

Yet despite his success, Paige cannot play in the major leagues because he is black. Said Paige: "All the nice statements in the world ain't gonna knock down Jim Crow."

1942 IN JANUARY, MR. WALKER JENNINGS PASSES ON.

ALL OF TUCKWILLA ATTENDS HIS FUNERAL.

HIS TWIN SONS, LONG RETURNED FROM PLAYIN' TWO YEARS FOR A CARDINALS MINOR LEAGUE TEAM, CLAIM THEIR INHERITANCE.

MR. JENNINGS WASN'T A WARMHEARTED MAN, BUT YOU ALWAYS KNEW WHERE YOU STOOD, WHEN HIS FENCE BROKE AND HIS STOCK STARTED EATIN' MY CROP, HE'D FIX THAT FENCE RIGHT AWAY,

THEM BOYS WILL LET THEIR STOCK EAT ALL YOUR GARDEN UP BEFORE THEY GET OFF THEIR HORSES AND FIX WHAT BELONGS TO THEM.

SO I FIX THEIR FENCE MYSELF,

THEM JENNINGS TWINS DO NOTHIN' FOR YOU EXCEPT GET INTO YOUR BUSINESS LOOKING FOR FAULTS AND FAILURES.

"YOU MAKIN' THOSE ROWS WIDE ENOUGH? FOUR FEET?"

FOUR FEET ON THIS THIN LAND? YOU CAN'T GO FOUR FEET ON THIS THIN LAND.

DURIN' PLANTIN': "YOU LAYIN' DOWN TOO MUCH FERTILIZER, EMMET."

EVEN MY BOY KNOWS IF YOU DON'T LAY DOWN ENOUGH GUANO, YOUR COTTON DON'T GET UP AND GET.

I JUST HUMBLE DOWN: "THAT'S SOMETHIN' TO THINK ABOUT, MR. WILLIAM."

THEN I JUST KEEP ON DOIN' THINGS THE WAY I KNOW HOW TO DO THEM.

SOON AS THAT COTTON IS READY TO BE PICKED, THE TUCKWILLA SCHOOL BOARD ALWAYS RUNS OUT OF MONEY.

NEVER SHUT DOWN THE WHITE SCHOOL. ALWAYS ENOUGH MONEY TO KEEP THEM OPEN. NEGRO EDUCATION BE DAMNED.

WE TAKE UP A COLLECTION FOR THE TEACHER TO KEEP TEACHIN'. SOME YEARS IT AIN'T MORE THAN CORN, CABBAGE, AND SIDE MEAT.

AIN'T GONNA KEEP MY BOY DOWN LIKE THAT AS LONG AS THERE'S A TEACHER WILLIN' TO TEACH.

ON A GOOD DAY I CAN PUT 100 LBS. OF COTTON IN A SACK. FRANCES, MY COUSINS FLOYD AND BUSTER, THEY HELP OUT TOO.

THEM JENNINGS TWINS, THEY KEEP COMIN'
ROUND. "WHERE YOUR BOY AT, EMMET?"

"GETTIN' HIS LESSONS, MR. WILLIAM."

I STAY SHUT MOUTHED AND KEEP PICKIN'
AND SAY NO MORE ABOUT THE MATTER.

THE NEXT DAY THE JENNINGS TWINS CATCH UP WITH EMMET, JR. AND A FEW OF
HIS PALS OVER BY WICKAHIKEN CREEK AND CALL IT TRESPASSIN'. THEM TWINS
OWN MOST OF TUCKWILLA -- WALKIN' OUT YOUR DOOR IS TRESPASSIN' IF THEY
CHOOSE TO CALL IT THAT.

THEY CAME DOWN OFF THEIR HORSES AND TOOK A STRAP TO THEM BOYS.

EMMET, JR. COME HOME ALL ROUGHED UP. FRANCES IS SCARED. WHAT HAPPENED TO LUCAS CRUTCHFIELD IS STILL FRESH IN EVERYONE'S MIND.

NEXT DAY THEY BACK. "WHERE YOUR BOY AT, EMMET? BOY RAISED RIGHT SHOULD BE HELPIN' HIS DADDY."

I DON'T TAKE OFF MY HAT. I MENTION NOTHING ABOUT HIS LESSONS, EITHER. "BE JOININ' ME SOON, MR. WALLACE."

I HUMBLE DOWN AGAIN, BUT KEEP ON DOIN' THINGS THE WAY I SEE BEST TO DO THEM.

NEXT FEW DAYS THE TWINS COME ROUND, THEY KEEP THEIR DISTANCE AND I KEEP MINE. I KNOW WHAT THEY WAITIN' TO SEE.

FEW MORE DAYS PASS LIKE THIS TILL FINALLY THEY RIDE OVER.

"WHERE YOUR BOY AT, EMMET?"

THERE WAS PLENTY OF ANGER IN ME BUT I HOLD MY TONGUE. WHAT ELSE WAS I TO DO? CRY ABOUT MY RIGHTS? TELL THEM I AM BEIN' MISTREATED?

YOU DO THAT, AND YOU DIE NO DIFFERENT THAN LUCAS CRUTCHFIELD.

TUESDAY THE FOLLOWING WEEK, EMMET, JR. IS COMING HOME AFTER FETCHING A FEW FRYERS FROM ELMER BETTIS FOR OUR DINNER.

BY THE TIME EMMET, JR. SAW 'EM, IT WAS TOO LATE. HE DIDN'T MAKE IT HOME IN TIME FOR DINNER.

FRANCES KNEW RIGHT AWAY THAT SOMETHIN' WAS TERRIBLY WRONG. BOY WASN'T EVEN AN HOUR LATE, AND SHE KNEW.

I HEADED TOWARD ELMER'S PLACE AS FAST AS MY GIMPY LEG WOULD CARRY ME.

"EMMET, JR. COME AND GONE ABOUT TWO HOURS AGO," ELMER SAYS.

I MAKE A FEW MORE INQUIRIES, BUT NO ONE HAD SEEN EMMET, JR.

I HEADED HOME AND SAW CECIL BROWN'S WAGON PARKED OUT FRONT. SOMETHIN' IRREGULAR GOIN' ON, CECIL BROWN NEVER CALLED ON US BEFORE. HE NOT THE VISITIN' TYPE.

CECIL WAS 'RIDIN' RIGHT PAST CARSON CROSSING AND SAW ONE OF THEM FRYERS LAYIN' IN THE ROAD.

THEN HE HEARD SOME RUSTLIN' IN THE GRASS. THOUGHT IT WAS A FOX OR MAYBE A WILD PIG. HE GOT OFF HIS WAGON TO TAKE A LOOK.

HE FOUND EMMET, JR. WITH HIS HANDS TRUSSED BEHIND HIS BACK AND A COTTON SACK TIED AROUND HIS HEAD, BLOOD LEAKIN' THROUGH THE SACK.

40

FOR THE REST OF THE EVENIN' THINGS WERE REAL QUIET AROUND THE HOUSE.

FRANCES AND I HARDLY SPOKE A WORD BETWEEN US WHILE SHE TENDED TO EMMET, JR.

HIS INJURIES WEREN'T AS BAD AS WE'D FEARED. MOST OF THE BLOOD BELONGED TO THE CHICKEN.

NEXT TIME, THAT MIGHT NOT BE THE CASE.

NEXT MORNIN', EMMET, JR. JOINS ME IN THE FIELD PICKIN' COTTON.

1943 EACH AND EVERY SUNDAY MORNIN' SINCE I STOPPED PLAYIN' BALL, FRANCES INSISTED I ATTEND CHURCH. SHE WORRIES ABOUT ME IN THIS LIFE AND THE NEXT.

I LISTEN TO PASTOR WILLS PREACHIN'. I HEAR THE SPIRITUALS. I SEE THEM WORDS AND THEM HYMNS TOUCHIN' PEOPLE ON THE INSIDE. BUT THEY DON'T TOUCH MY INSIDE.

EACH AND EVERY SUNDAY, THE CONGREGATION WALKS DOWN TO THE RIVER. EACH AND EVERY WEEK, PASTOR WILLS SHOUTS OUT, "WHO WILL BE CLEANSED BY JESUS? WHO WILL LET JESUS WASH AWAY THEIR TROUBLES? WHO WILL LET JESUS WASH AWAY ALL THEIR PAIN AND ANGER?"

EACH AND EVERY WEEK I STAY PUT.

IF THE RIVER WASHED AWAY ALL MY PAIN AND ANGER, THERE WOULD BE NOTHING LEFT.

1944

BASEBALL
SATCHEL PAIGE
ALL-STARS
— vs. —
TUCKWILLA ALL-STARS
SATURDAY, SEPT. 2
AT 2:00 P.M.
JENNINGS
PARK
CHILDREN 20¢ ADULTS 50¢

FEATURING PITCHING LEGEND SATCHEL PAIGE

NEVER SEEN A CROWD SO BIG IN TUCKWILLA. THEY'RE COMIN' FROM AS FAR AWAY AS DANVILLE AND LYME. EMMET, JR., LIKE EVERY BLACK BOY IN ALABAMA, WORSHIPS SATCHEL PAIGE.

FRANCES WAS GOIN' TO BRING EMMET, JR. HERE TODAY--THEN HER SISTER TOOK ILL AND SHE HAD TO CARE FOR HER. I WOULD NOT HAVE BEEN HERE OTHERWISE. BASEBALL REMINDS ME OF THINGS I'D RATHER NOT THINK ABOUT.

BOY HAS SOME NOTION THAT I ONCE PLAYED BALL. BUT HE DIDN'T HEAR IT FROM ME. I DON'T TALK ABOUT MY DAYS AS A BALLPLAYER. IT'S LIKE TALKIN' ABOUT A DEAD MAN.

THEM TWINS SPENT A FEW DOLLARS TRYIN' TO MAKE JENNINGS FIELD INTO A REAL BALLPARK, SHADED GRANDSTAND FOR WHITES AND A DUGOUT FOR THE HOME TEAM.

EVERYONE TURNIN' OUT TODAY, EVEN CLARA COLES, OLDEST PERSON IN ALL OF TUCKWILLA.

EMMET, JR. AND I FIND US A SEAT.

NO SIGN OF PAIGE, BUT THE REST OF HIS TEAM IS HERE. SOME OF 'EM STRETCHIN' OUT, OTHERS CATCHIN' A FEW WINKS, LIKELY TIRED FROM AN ALL-NIGHT BUS RIDE. THEY ALL LOOK FAMILIAR, BUT I DON'T RECOGNIZE ANY OF 'EM.

TUCKWILLA TEAM IS ON THE FIELD, WARMIN' UP. THEM I RECOGNIZE.

THE TWINS, OF COURSE.

CHRISTIAN DOOLEY OWNS THE LUMBER MILL, HOWARD GIBBS IS THE SHERIFF.

OSCAR OWENS, HE HERE TOO. HE AIN'T FROM TUCKWILLA. BORN AND RAISED IN MOBILE.

PEOPLE SAY HE THE BEST PLAYER IN THE SOUTH. PLAYED FOR CHICAGO WHITE STOCKINGS TILL THEY KICKED HIM OUT OF THE LEAGUE FOR STABBIN' AN UMPIRE AFTER A GAME.

JUST ABOUT GAME TIME, AND STILL NO SIGN OF PAIGE.
HIS TEAM TAKES THE FIELD FOR THEIR WARM-UPS.

A BATTER HITS A BALL TO THE INFIELDERS,
STARTIN' WITH THE THIRD BASEMAN..

HE MAKES THE PLAY, DIVIN' TO HIS
RIGHT ...

AND COMES UP THROWIN' FROM HIS KNEES.

THE FIRST BASEMAN, STRETCHIN' ABOUT AS FAR AS HE CAN GO, SCOOPS UP THE THROW OUT OF THE DIRT.

ALL THE INFIELDERS GET INTO THE ACT NOW: BARE-HANDED PICKUPS...

SOMERSAULTIN' THROWS... EMMET, JR. IS AMAZED BY THE ACROBATICS.

I POINT OUT THEY JUST PUTTIN' ON A SHOW, PLAYIN' SHADOW BALL -- BASEBALL WITHOUT A BALL.

"THEY JUST TRICKIN' YOU, BOY. IT AIN'T REAL."

JENNINGS TWINS, THEY AIN'T AMUSED,
THEY WEARIN' THEIR GAME FACES.

THEY HEAD OVER TO HOME PLATE TO
HAVE A WORD WITH THE BATTER, THEY
SURELY PAID A PRETTY PENNY TO GET
PAIGE HERE, AND THEY WANT TO KNOW
WHERE HE AT.

A HALF HOUR PASSES.

WITH A CROWD GROWIN' RESTLESS AND
THE TWINS NOT WANTIN' TO REFUND
ANY TICKETS, THEY DECIDE TO START
WITHOUT PAIGE.

MAE BELLOWS AND MARION WERTH, TUCKWILLA'S TWO WHITE WAR WIDOWS,
STAND AT HOME PLATE AND SING THE NATIONAL ANTHEM.

WILLIAM JENNINGS TAKES THE MOUND AND KICKS THE DIRT THIS WAY AND THAT, GETTIN' IT JUST SO.

TAKES A FEW WARM-UP PITCHES.

THE COLORED TEAM LEAD HITTER STANDS A FEW FEET FROM THE PLATE, TAKIN' SOME SWINGS.

GAME YET TO BEGIN AND EMMET, JR.'S EYES GLUED TO THAT BASEBALL DIAMOND. IT'S MORE THAN THE BIG CROWD THAT HAS HIM EXCITED.

FOR THE FIRST TIME IN HIS LIFE, HE SEEIN' A BLACK MAN GOIN' HEAD-TO-HEAD WITH A WHITE MAN, NOT JUST ANY WHITE MAN EITHER, BUT ONE OF THE JENNINGS TWINS.

THE UMPIRE YELLS, "PLAY BALL!"

LEADOFF HITTER, SHORT FELLA, STEPS INTO BATTER'S BOX. BATS LEFTY.

TAKES THE FIRST PITCH. "STRIKE ONE."

HOMETOWN UMP HAS A GENEROUS STRIKE ZONE. NEXT PITCH IS INSIDE AND IS ALSO CALLED A STRIKE.

HITTER, WITH TWO STRIKES ON HIM, NOW STARTS SWINGIN' AT ANYTHIN' CLOSE, FOULS OFF TWO PITCHES.

CRACK

ON THE FIFTH PITCH HE GOES DOWN SWINGIN'.

BASEBALL IS WON AND LOST ON THE LITTLE THINGS. DETAILS THAT MOST PEOPLE WON'T EVER NOTICE UNLESS THEY LOOKIN' FOR IT, LIKE A HITTER CHOKIN' UP ON THE BAT AFTER TWO STRIKES,

OR HOW A PITCHER MAY TELEGRAPH HIS PITCHES BY DIPPIN' A SHOULDER OR THE WAY HE GRIPS A BALL.

AS THE GAME GOES ON, I START POINTIN' THESE THINGS OUT TO MY BOY, AND BEFORE I REALIZE IT, I AM PULLED BACK INTO THE GAME. IT'S LIKE FEELIN' A LIMB THAT YOU THOUGHT YOU LOST.

IN THE SECOND INNING, NEGRO TEAM LEADOFF MAN DRAGS A BUNT.

THEN A HIT-AND-RUN. SHORTSTOP COVERS SECOND AND THE GROUND BALL IS SMACKED RIGHT WHERE HE USUALLY AT.

RUNNER GOIN' ALL THE WAY TO THIRD ON THE PLAY,

NEXT, A DELAYED DOUBLE STEAL.
CATCHER THROWS TO SECOND.

RUNNER SLIDES IN SAFE AS BALL
BOUNCES OFF HIS SHOULDER.

RUNNER ON THIRD COMES HOME TO
SCORE.

NEXT BATTER PUSHES A GROUNDER TO
SECOND. IT'S THE FIRST OUT, BUT IT
ALLOWS THE RUNNER ON SECOND TO
MOVE OVER TO THIRD.

NEXT BATTER HITS A POP FLY TO
THE CENTER FIELDER FOR THE SECOND
OUT.

THE RUNNER ON THIRD TAGS AND
SCORES -- TWO RUNS ON A COUPLE
OF WEAK SINGLES! THAT'S THE
NEGRO GAME! FASTER, MORE
AGGRESSIVE THAN THE WHITE GAME.

IN THE FOURTH INNING, TUCKWILLA STARTS FLEXIN' THEIR MUSCLES.

AFTER TWO OUTS, DOOLEY RIPS A DOUBLE DOWN THE LINE...

MR. WALLACE GETS A HOLD OF ONE NEXT.

HITS A MAMMOTH HOME RUN.

OUTFIELDERS DON'T BOTHER TO GO BACK ON IT. THEY KNOW IT'S GONE.

MR. WILLIAM UP NEXT.

HE TEARS INTO THAT BALL AND SENDS IT INTO THE CORNER FOR A STAND-UP DOUBLE.

COLORED PITCHER STARTIN' TO DROOP WITH TUCKWILLA'S BEST HITTER STEPPIN' UP.

OSCAR OWENS.

FIRST PITCH TO HIM IS HIT OFF THE TOP OF THE BAT AND HIT A MILE HIGH.

THE SHORTSTOP STARTS IMMEDIATELY SCREAMIN', "I GOT IT! I GOT IT!"

MR. WILLIAM HESITATES FOR A MOMENT AT SECOND BASE...

...AS THE BALL BOUNCES OFF THE OUTFIELD FENCE AND IS PLAYED BY THE LEFT FIELDER.

MR. WILLIAM, REALIZIN' HE BEEN TRICKED, NOW TAKES OFF.

LEFT FIELDER GETS RID OF IT QUICK AS MR. WILLIAM, NOW IN FULL STRIDE, IS AROUND THIRD HEADIN' FOR HOME.

THE THROW EASILY BEATS MR. WILLIAM...

WHO'S COMIN' INTO HOME HARD, HOPIN' TO KNOCK THE BALL LOOSE.

THUD

CATCHER HOLDS ON TO THE BALL, AND THE INNING IS OVER.

THE NEXT FEW INNINGS ARE PLAYED HARD. MR. WILLIAM PITCHIN' BATTERS INSIDE AND TIGHT.

WHEN THE SHORTSTOP WHO FOOLED HIM COMES TO BAT, HE GETS PLUNKED WITH A FASTBALL.

SHORTSTOP GOT NO GET-BACK IN HIM! HE STEALS SECOND AND THIRD!

MR. WILLIAM, THOUGH, HE GETTIN' STRONGER AS THE GAME GOES ON. STRIKES OUT THE SIDE.

ENTERING THE BOTTOM OF THE EIGHTH INNING, TUCKWILLA IS DOWN 6 RUNS TO 3. HOW I WANT TO SEE THAT SCORE HOLD.

	1	2	3	4	5	6	7	8	9		
VISITORS	0	2	1	2	0	0	1	0			6
TUCKWILLA	0	0	0	2	0	1	0				3

THE COLORED PITCHER AIN'T GETTIN' THE SAME MOVEMENT ON HIS PITCHES ...

... AND TUCKWILLA IS HITTIN' HIM HARD.

THE FIRST THREE BATTERS ALL GET HITS.

THE FIRST HITTER IS COMIN' AROUND TO SCORE,

KEEP EXPECTIN' THE PITCHER TO BE PULLED. BUT AS DROOPY AS HE IS, HE STAYS IN THE GAME. IT'S LIKELY THE TEAM PROBABLY PLAYED A DOUBLEHEADER YESTERDAY AND HAS ANOTHER GAME TONIGHT. TEAM AIN'T GONNA WASTE ANOTHER ARM ON THIS GAME.

BATTER STEPS UP TO THE PLATE.

FIRST PITCH AIN'T NEAR THE STRIKE ZONE.

THE SECOND PITCH IS IN THE DIRT, THE CATCHER MAKES A GOOD PLAY TO KEEP THE BALL FROM GETTIN' PAST 'EM.

THIRD PITCH IS A BREAKIN' BALL THAT DON'T BREAK.

CRACK

ANOTHER RUN SCORES. TUCKWILLA IS WITHIN' ONE, AND STILL NO OUTS.

HOWARD GIBBS STEPS INTO THE BATTER'S BOX. HE SMELLS BLOOD AND IS READY TO TAKE HIS CUTS.

BUT THE PITCHER, HE AIN'T LOOKIN' AT THE CATCHER'S MITT.

NO ONE AT JENNINGS FIELD IS LOOKIN' AT THE BATTER OR THE PITCHER.

ALL EYES ARE ON THE MAIN ENTRANCE BY THE GRANDSTAND.

SATCHEL PAIGE HAS ARRIVED.

PAIGE WORKS THE MOUND TO HIS LIKIN'...

GIBBS AND THE UMPIRE WAITIN' ON PAIGE TO TAKE HIS WARM-UPS, CATCHER IN HIS CROUCH,

PAIGE DON'T MOVE, HE WAITIN' ON THE BATTER, HE READY TO PITCH!

STRIKE ONE!

NEXT PITCH SAME AS THE FIRST, MAYBE A HAIR OUTSIDE.

UMP CALLS IT A BALL.

PAIGE SMILES EAR-TO-EAR, STEPS OFF THE MOUND AND HAS A FEW WORDS FOR THE UMP. ANOTHER FIRST FOR EMMET, JR.: SEEIN' A BLACK MAN SASS A WHITE.

AFTER JAWIN' FOR ANOTHER MINUTE, PAIGE STEPS BACK ONTO THE MOUND.

AIN'T A PERSON IN THE CROWD NOT PAYIN' ATTENTION. ANYTHIN' IS NOW POSSIBLE.

THE NEXT PITCH IS A BIG BREAKIN' CURVEBALL THAT IS SWUNG AT AND MISSED. ONE BALL, TWO STRIKES.

PAIGE'S NEXT PITCH IS ANOTHER FAST-BALL, AND GIBBS STROKES IT BETWEEN THIRD AND SHORT.

A RUN COMES IN, AND THE GAME IS TIED.

THE TUCKWILLA DUGOUT CELEBRATIN'!

PAIGE DON'T SEEM PARTICULARLY BOTHERED BY IT. HE WALKS OVER TO FIRST BASE TO CONGRATULATE GIBBS FOR GETTIN' A HIT OFF HIM.

GIBBS NEVER SHOOK A BLACK MAN'S HAND BEFORE, AND HE AIN'T STARTIN' NOW.

NEXT HITTER IS DOOLEY.

PAIGE'S FIRST PITCH IS A FASTBALL RIGHT BY HIM.

NEXT PITCH IS ANOTHER ONE.

THIS ONE IS HIT, THOUGH.

THE THIRD BASEMAN STABS AT IT, BUT IT RICOCHETS OFF THE HEEL OF HIS GLOVE.

THE SHORTSTOP QUICKLY COLLECTS THE BALL IN SHALLOW LEFT FIELD, TOO LATE TO MAKE A PLAY AT FIRST.

BASES ARE LOADED, AND BOTH BATTERS WHO FACED PAIGE HAVE GOTTEN HITS OFF HIM. PAIGE MAY NOT LOOK ANY OLDER, BUT HE AIN'T GOT NEAR THE SAME FASTBALL HE ONCE DID. I CAN'T HELP BUT WONDER IF THIS MAN CAN STILL PITCH, OR IF HE JUST ALL SHOW.

SOME TAUNTIN' COMIN' FROM THE TUCKWILLA BENCH. IF PAIGE HEARS, IT DON'T BOTHER HIM NONE.

HE STILL LOOKIN' FOR LAUGHS. HE WALKS OVER TO THE THIRD BASEMAN. PAIGE CHECKS TO SEE IF THERE'S A HOLE IN HIS MITT.

MR. WALLACE STEPS UP TO THE PLATE.

RUNNERS TAKE THEIR LEAD OFF THE BASES.

PAIGE HASN'T TAKEN THE MOUND--HE STILL JAWIN' TO HIS THIRD BASEMAN. JUST AS I REMEMBER, EVERYTHIN' REVOLVIN' AROUND PAIGE. HOWEVER BIG THE GAME, PAIGE IS BIGGER.

MR. WALLACE, HE GETTIN' STEAMED! BARKS SOMETHIN' AT PAIGE.

PAIGE HAS GOT HIS GOAT! COLORED SECTION HOOTIN' AND LAUGHIN'.

PAIGE STEPS TOWARD THE PLATE. STILL PLAYIN' THINGS FOR LAUGHS. PRETENDS HE CAN'T HEAR.

MR. WALLACE WALKS A FOOT TOWARD THE MOUND.

HE YELLS AGAIN. THIS TIME IT IS LOUD ENOUGH FOR EVERYONE TO HEAR,

PITCH THE BALL, YOU WASHED-UP NIGGER!

PAIGE TURNS HIS BACK TO THE PLATE AND GESTURES TO HIS FIELDERS.

THE OUTFIELDERS JOG IN...

AND TAKE A SEAT WITH THE INFIELDERS BEHIND SECOND BASE.

PAIGE RECLAIMS THE MOUND.

THE CATCHER SQUATS BEHIND THE PLATE.

MR. WALLACE HESITATES BEFORE STEPPIN' INTO THE BATTER'S BOX, AND EXCHANGES WORDS WITH HIS BROTHER IN THE ON-DECK CIRCLE.

MR. WILLIAM SHOUTS SOMETHIN' AT THE MOUND.

WHATEVER WAS SAID, PAIGE DON'T ACKNOWLEDGE IT. CLOWNIN' TIME IS OVER, HE ALL BUSINESS NOW.

TUCKWILLA DUGOUT IS ON ITS FEET KICKIN' UP A FUSS, THINKIN' PAIGE IS PLAYIN' MORE GAMES. WHAT THEY SHOUTIN', I'D RATHER NOT REPEAT.

PAIGE JUST WAITS.

MR. WALLACE STEPS INTO THE BATTER'S BOX, REFUSIN' TO BE SHOWN UP. ALL HE HAS TO DO IS PUT THE BALL IN PLAY, AND EVERY RUN SCORES.

THAT BALL WAS MOVIN' SO FAST I COULDN'T EVEN SEE IT. IF I DIDN'T KNOW BETTER, I'D A THOUGHT THEY WAS PLAYIN' SHADOW BALL.

NEXT PITCH SAME AS THE FIRST.

MR. WALLACE GOES DOWN ON THREE PITCHES.

PAIGE GETS THE BALL BACK AND
WASTES NO TIME GETTIN' READY.

MR. WILLIAM STEPS UP TO THE PLATE.

THREE MORE PITCHES,
AND MR. WILLIAM STRIKES OUT
JUST LIKE HIS BROTHER.

NEXT BATTER, OSCAR OWENS, STANDS IN.

AFTER TAKIN' A PITCH FOR A STRIKE, HE TRYS TO BUNT.

YOU KNOW YOU LICKED WHEN YOUR CLEANUP HITTER IS BUNTIN'. OWENS NEVER MAKES CONTACT. GOES DOWN ON THREE PITCHES TOO, INNING OVER.

WHOOSH!

THE CROWD IS ON THEIR FEET, CHEERIN'. NOT JUST THE COLORED SECTION, EITHER.

PAIGE AIN'T JAWIN' NO MORE,
IN NINE PITCHES HE SAID WHAT HE HAD TO SAY.

THE LAST INNIN' IS AN AFTERTHOUGHT. DON'T ASK ME THE FINAL SCORE.
I COULDN'T TELL YOU.

PAIGE DOESN'T EVEN RETURN TO THE MOUND IN THE NINTH. BY THE TIME
THE GAME ENDED, HE WAS PROBABLY WELL ON HIS WAY TO THE NEXT GAME,
HIS NEXT PAYCHECK, TUCKWILLA JUST ANOTHER GIG.

EMMET, JR. AND I WALKED HOME TOGETHER, MY BOY AS SPIRITED AS I'VE SEEN HIM FOR SOME TIME, STOPPIN' EVERY SO OFTEN TO APE SATCHEL'S HERKY-JERKY WINDUP.

I'M STILL LIMPIN' ALONG, BUT I GOT A BOUNCE IN MY STEP, TOO.

I THOUGHT HARD ABOUT THEM JENNINGS TWINS, HOW IT CAME TO BE THAT THESE MEN LORDED OVER US. HOW DO MEN SO SMALL GET SO LARGE? WHO MADE IT SO?

YOU LIVE UNDER THEIR RULIN' FOR SO LONG THAT YOU SOON FORGET WHO YOU ARE, WHAT YOU CAN BE.

THAT EVENIN' AFTER SUPPER, EMMET, JR. AND I RETIRED TO THE PORCH, AND I SHOWED HIM SOMETHIN' I HAD HID AWAY FOR MANY YEARS.

IT WAS THE BASEBALL GIVEN TO ME BY SATCHEL PAIGE.

FOR THE FIRST TIME, I TOLD EMMET, JR. THE STORY OF HOW HIS DADDY WENT HEAD-TO-HEAD WITH SATCHEL PAIGE.

AND UNLIKE THEM TUCKWILLA BOYS,

HIS DADDY CAME OUT ON TOP.

CRACK

FOR THE FIRST TIME SINCE I PLAYED BALL, SINCE EMMET, JR. WAS A BABY, I FELT SOMETHIN' ON THE INSIDE. I REMEMBERED THE TYPE OF MAN I AM.

I GAVE EMMET, JR. THAT BALL ... I HOPE IT REMINDS HIM OF WHO HE CAN BE.

THE END

Striking Out Jim Crow
Panel Discussions

PAGE 1: *Wages*
In 1929, black sharecroppers earned about forty to fifty cents a day. A maid, working seven days a week, might bring in four dollars for the week. Some of the better Negro League ballplayers were paid $275 per month. That's what Paige made playing for the Birmingham Black Barons in 1929. After the stock market crash of 1929, signaling the Great Depression, these wages fell.

PAGE 2: *The Railroad*
From 1900 to 1945 was the Golden Age of the railroad. Ninety-eight percent of all travel between cities in 1916 was by train. It wasn't until the 1930s that the automobile cut into the rail passenger market.

By 1920, 100,000 travelers per night were sleeping in Pullman sleepers. The Pullman Company was the largest employer of Negroes in America. The service provided by the African American Pullman porters was legendary and within African American communities the Pullman porters were held in high regard. In 1937, the Brotherhood of Sleeping Car Porters, under the leadership of A. Philip Randolph, was finally recognized as the porters' official union by the Pullman Company after a long and often bitter struggle. Their fight for better working conditions helped lay the foundation for the civil rights movement.

The sound of a locomotive's whistle could be heard in the homes of most Americans. Lumber, steel, refrigerators, milk, newspapers—the railroad shipped almost every product consumed in America. A train whistle might also signal the arrival of the circus, traveling theater shows, vaudeville acts, and, of course, sports teams.

PAGE 2: *Sharecropper Shacks*
Poorly constructed sharecropper shacks were usually built on the landowner's property and leased back to the sharecropper. Rent was subtracted from the sharecropper's wages. Landowners would also charge for use of tools, equipment, and even food. Despite working the land the whole year, the sharecropper would often find himself in debt to the landowner.

PAGE 3: *The Negro National League*
The Negro National League was the first all-black league to last more than one season. It was started in 1920 by Rube Foster, former star pitcher and owner-manager of the Chicago American Giants. In 1929, the league included the Chicago American Giants, Cuban Stars, Detroit Stars, Kansas City Monarchs, Birmingham Black Barons, and Memphis Red Sox. The league folded in 1931, another victim of the Great Depression.

PAGE 4: *African American Press*
If you were looking in the 1920s for articles about black businesses, sports figures, or cultural figures, you'd find virtually no mention of them in the majority of newspapers. Like the rest of the country, the newspaper industry was segregated. The *Chicago Defender, Pittsburgh Courier*, and the Baltimore *Afro-American* were three of the country's most widely circulated black newspapers. The newspapers were read throughout the country. Black Pullman porters carried the papers south across the Mason-Dixon Line. The papers advocated for better working and living conditions for blacks throughout the country.

The sports pages in African American papers fought for integration years before Jackie Robinson broke baseball's color barrier in 1947.

PAGE 4: *Bullet Rogan*
It was not until he was thirty, after more than nine years of playing on U.S. Army teams, that Wilber "Bullet" Joe Rogan began his Negro Leagues career with the Kansas City Monarchs. His devastating fastball, along with a dazzling array of forkballs, palm balls, spitballs, and curves, made him one of the League's most dominant pitchers. Rogan also played as an outfielder and led the Negro National League in 1922 with sixteen home runs.

PAGE 5: *Paige's Personal Catcher*
Albany, Georgia, native Bill Perkins was Satchel Paige's personal catcher throughout his career. He was a strong defensive catcher and wore a chest protector emblazoned with the words *Thou shalt not steal!* As Satchel jumped from team to team, he would insist that Perkins be signed along with him. In 1948, the year Paige made it to the major leagues, Perkins was shot and killed in a restaurant.

PAGE 13: *Paige's Pitches*
Paige was a brilliant self-promoter. He even promoted his pitches by giving them names! They included the Jump Ball, Bee Ball, Hesitation, Nothing Ball, Hurry-up Ball, Drop Ball, Bat Dodger, the Midnight Creeper, and Four-day Rider.

Page 15: Rituals and Rhythms
Ballplayers from all sports often engage in rituals and routines as a way to combat distractions and focus their attention. For example, a basketball player, before shooting a free throw, may always lift a hand toward the basket and then dribble the ball three times. The Yankee all-star

shortstop Derek Jeter compulsively tugs at both his batting gloves as he steps out of the batter's box between every pitch of an at-bat.

PAGE 19: *Speed and Daring*
The Negro League games, as opposed to those of the white major leagues, stressed aggressive base running. Teams did not sit around waiting for home runs but rather forced the action with hit-and-runs, suicide squeezes, and double steals. Opposing teams felt that Satchel Paige's delivery made it easy to steal bases. As a power pitcher with a high leg kick, he gave runners more of a head start when they were trying to swipe a base.

PAGE 24: *Barnstorming*
Barnstorming was a popular form of entertainment in the 1920s, in which stunt pilots would perform tricks with airplanes, flying from town to town, often landing in farmers' fields by the barns. The term *barnstorming* also became linked with sports teams, especially baseball. Teams caravaned by motorcar or bus over dirt roads, traveling hundreds of miles each day. Day games were often followed by a night game in the next county, followed by a doubleheader the next afternoon 500 miles away.

Life on the road was rough going for black barnstormers. Most hotels wouldn't give them rooms, forcing them to sleep on buses, in barns, or in stadiums. Players would travel to play exhibition games against white and other black teams to earn extra income beyond what their teams paid them. The games against whites were cash cows, often drawing thousands of fans to these small towns to witness the great Negro League players.

PAGES 24, 26: *The 1934 St. Louis Cardinals*
In 1934, the St. Louis Cardinals were the Major League Baseball World Series champions. Their nickname was "The Gas House Gang," due to the team's generally shabby appearance and rough-and-tumble tactics. The team boasted

stars like Joe Medwick, Ripper Collins, Pepper Martin, and pitcher Dizzy Dean. The 1934 Cardinals won ninety-five games and beat the Detroit Tigers in seven games to win the World Series. Dean made more money barnstorming with Paige for a summer than he did all season playing for the Cardinals.

PAGE 33: *Jim Crow's Unwritten Laws*
Jim Crow laws throughout the South enforced racial segregation. Some of the laws, such as poll taxes and literacy tests to suppress minority voters, were written, and other laws were assumed. Decades of manners and customs, left over from the days of slavery, calcified into an etiquette, "humbling down": taking off your hat, using the back entrance of homes. This "etiquette" was demanded by whites, and to ignore it would mean risking your life. Blacks were often killed for just looking at a white woman or talking back to a white person.

PAGE 37: *Lynching*
In the last decades of the nineteenth century, the lynching of black people in the Southern and border states became a method used by whites to terrorize blacks. A uniquely American institution, lynching was the public murder of individuals suspected of "crimes," conceived and carried out by a mob. A lynching was a local community event. There were even postcards sold as mementos. Most often, lynchings were by hanging or shooting. Many were of a more heinous variety—burning at the stake, maiming, dismemberment, castration, and other forms of physical torture.

Southern politicians and officials often supported "lynch law," and came to power on a platform of white supremacy. State authorities often attempted to prevent lynchings, but seldom punished the mob participants. In *The Tragedy of Lynching* (1933), the sociologist Arthur F. Raper estimated, from his study of one hundred lynchings, that "at least one-half of the lynchings are carried out with police officers participating, and that in nine-tenths of the others the officers either condone or wink at the mob action."

PAGE 44: *The Role of Church*
Churches were a vital social institution and central to the African American community. Church revivals were great religious and social events. For sharecroppers, the church was the one place, besides the fields, they could congregate in large numbers. Gospels and hymns were sung with lyrics that praised the Lord, asked for the strength to persevere, and begged for deliverance and redemption.

Some churches became centers for political activity, leading the charge for improving housing, health care, and education. Like many of today's churches, they also provided charitable assistance, including food distribution and covering the costs of funerals. Relatives who lived elsewhere would send money to a church's minister to pass along instead of sending it directly to their family, fearing (with good reason) the property owner would take it.

The congregation depicted in this scene is from a Baptist church. Other denominations (such as the Methodists) performed their baptisms with a symbolic sprinkle of water. The Baptists, using John's baptism in the river Jordan as a model, favored full immersion.

PAGE 66: *Paige Has Arrived*
Paige rarely let a signed contract dictate where he should play, especially if a more lucrative offer was made. As a result, Paige routinely missed scheduled appearances. When he did arrive, he was often late. Paige may have walked slowly, but he drove fast, and being a passenger in his car meant risking your life. One time, already late to a game, Paige was pulled over for speeding. He was taken to a local judge and fined forty dollars. Paige handed the judge eighty dollars and said, "Here ya go, Mr. Judge, 'cause I'm coming back through tomorrow."

Page 74: *The N-Word*
"Out on the field, there'd be some white

folks in the stands," Satchel Paige said in his autobiography, *Maybe I'll Pitch Forever.* "Some of them'd call you [the N-word], but most would cheer you."

PAGE 75: *Calling in the Infielders*
Paige enhanced the intrinsic drama of baseball by injecting his own stunts. Calling in the fielders, a dramatic gesture, was a routine Paige performed many times. Paige's most legendary stunt occurred in the 1942 Negro World Series, when he was facing off against his onetime teammate Josh Gibson, the most feared black hitter of his day. With the game on the line, Paige walked two hitters to load the bases in order to pitch to Gibson. The crowd went wild as Paige then struck out Gibson with three pitches.

PAGE 80: *His Next Gig*
Paige went on to pitch for another thirty years! All told, his pitching career spanned six decades. In 1948, the year after Jackie Robinson broke into the big leagues, the 42-year-old Paige was signed by the Cleveland Indians and helped them win a World Series. In 1953, while Paige was playing for the St. Louis Browns, New York Yankees manager, Casey Stengel, selected Paige for the All-Star team. In 1965, the 59-year-old Satchel Paige, pitching for the Kansas City A's, threw three scoreless innings against the Boston Red Sox. Satchel Paige was inducted into the Baseball Hall of Fame on August 2, 1971. He continued to barnstorm, ending his career with the Tulsa Oilers in 1976. Paige died in Kansas City in 1982.

Bibliography

Chafe, William Henry, Gavins, Raymond, and Korstad, Robert. *Remembering Jim Crow: African Americans Tell About Life in the Segregated South.* The New Press, New York, 2001.

Paige, Satchel and Lipman, David. *Maybe I'll Pitch Forever: A Great Baseball Player Tells the Hilarious Story Behind the Legend.* University of Nebraska Press, 1993.

Ribowsky, Mark. *Don't Look Back: Satchel Paige in the Shadows of Baseball.* Da Capo Press, New York, 1994.

Rosengarten, Theodore. *All God's Dangers: The Life of Nate Shaw.* Alfred A. Knopf, New York, 1975.

Credits

WRITER AND SERIES EDITOR

JAMES STURM is the cofounder and director of The Center for Cartoon Studies. His most recent graphic novel is *James Sturm's America.* His book *The Golem's Mighty Swing* was named "Best Comic 2001" by *Time* magazine. In 2004, his Marvel Comics graphic novel *Unstable Molecules* won the prestigious Eisner Award. James's writings and illustrations have appeared in the pages of *The Chronicle of Higher Education, The Onion, The New York Times,* and on the cover of *The New Yorker.*

ARTIST

RICH TOMMASO has been writing and drawing original comics and graphic novels for over ten years. He has worked for such publishers as Fantagraphics Books, Top Shelf Productions, Dark Horse Comics, Chronicle Books, and Alternative Comics. He has received accolades from many magazines and trade papers, including *Publishers Weekly, Spin* magazine, and *The Comics Journal.* Rich lives in Vermont.

INTRODUCTION

GERALD EARLY is a noted essayist and American culture critic and Director of the Center for Humanities at Washington University in St. Louis. Early is the author of several books, including *The Culture of Bruising: Essays on Prizefighting, Literature and Modern American Culture,* which won the 1994 National Book Critics Circle Award for criticism. He is also editor of numerous volumes, including *Body Language: Writers on Sports* (1998), *The Muhammad Ali Reader* (1998), *The Sammy Davis, Jr. Reader* (2001), and *Miles Davis and American Culture* (2001). He served as a consultant on Ken Burns's documentary films on baseball and jazz, both of which aired on PBS.